Rosicrucian Magic and Symbols

The Ultimate Guide to Rosicrucianism and Its Similarity to Occultism, Jewish Mysticism, Hermeticism, and Christian Gnosticism

Your Free Gift (only available for a limited time)

Thanks for getting this book! If you want to learn more about various spirituality topics, then join Mari Silva's community and get a free guided meditation MP3 for awakening your third eye. This guided meditation mp3 is designed to open and strengthen ones third eye so you can experience a higher state of consciousness. Simply visit the link below the image to get started.

https://spiritualityspot.com/meditation

Contents

Introduction

The Rosicrucians are a mystical society that has inspired fear and fascination for centuries. Most people know of the Rosicrucians through the mysterious symbolism in their secret documents.

The Rosicrucian Manifestos of the early seventeenth century describe the society as one that is part philosophical school, part scientific academy, part spiritual brotherhood, and part political party. Founded by Christian Rosenkreuz during the late fourteenth century, it was originally called the Order of the Rose Cross. It has been described as a lineage of initiates going as far back as Ancient Egypt or even Atlantis and linked to other secret societies such as Freemasonry.

This book will explore the mystery of Rosicrucianism, its symbolism, and its influence on modern secret societies. In the first chapter, we'll explain what Rosicrucianism is and give you the historical context of the society. The second chapter tells the story of Christian Rosenkreuz, the founder of Rosicrucianism. The third chapter covers the Egyptian and Hermetic origins of Rosicrucian symbolism and explains the Hermetic tradition as both a term and an esoteric system.

The fourth chapter provides a translation of an ancient Gnostic text called "Poimandres," which explains some of the symbolism of Rosicrucianism. The fifth chapter looks at the mystical Jewish tradition called Merkavah, which is closely linked to the mystery of the Holy Grail. The sixth chapter examines "Twenty-Two Paths of Enlightenment," a system used in a few of the ancient mystic schools to train the mind.

In the seventh chapter, we look at Alchemy and Kabbalah and their relationship to Rosicrucianism. Practical aspects of Rosicrucianism, including some meditations and rituals used, are discussed in the eighth chapter. The ninth chapter covers the daily life of a Rosicrucian, or someone who practices this philosophy, and offers various tips for meditation, grounding, shielding, and other facets.

This book has two surprise bonus chapters. The first will address the sixteen Secret Signs of the Rosicrucians as they were originally composed by a medical doctor and occultist Franz Hartmann, and the other bonus chapter will explain how one goes about joining a Rosicrucian order.

The mystery of the Rosicrucian Orders has attracted the attention of many modern esotericists. They have used this symbolism in their materials, claiming that they carry on a tradition going back to the founder of Rosicrucianism, Christian Rosenkreuz. This book aims to introduce Rosicrucian philosophy and practice so that those who have no previous knowledge may find it easier to make contact with the movement. It will be helpful for occultists, students, and anyone interested in learning more about Rosicrucianism.

Chapter 1: An Introduction to Rosicrucianism

Rosicrucianism is a philosophical and religious movement that originated in early 17th century Europe. The word *Rosicrucianism* comes from the Latin "Rosae Crucis," meaning "cross of the rose." The symbol of the cross within a rose is taken from a mystic legend about Christian Rosenkreuz. They were symbolized by a circle with a cross inscribed and were worn by followers often called Magi, or wise men. Rosicrucians are distinguished from other secret societies by their emphasis on esoteric knowledge. Rosicrucianism is characterized by its interest in alchemy, mysticism, magic, and various other occult sciences.

https://pixabay.com/de/photos/liebe-kreuzen-dornen-krone-herz-699480/

In this chapter, the reader will find an introduction to Rosicrucianism and its history. The information provided should serve as a base for further study on the subject. Bear in mind that the scope of this chapter does not allow for a comprehensive study on Rosicrucianism. It is intended as a starting point for the reader's interest or study.

The Definition of Rosicrucianism

Rosicrucianism is a form of esoteric Christian philosophy. It is believed to have been founded in late medieval Germany by Christian Rosenkreuz. The term "Rosicrucian" describes someone associated with this philosophical and religious movement, but this does not mean that such a person is involved in all aspects. For this reason, it is true that well-known individuals such as Carl Gustav Jung and Benjamin Franklin were not members of the original order but could still be classified as Rosicrucians.

This order started with Christian Rosenkreuz, who some believe was a real historical person, but there is doubt whether he was real or allegorical. One school of thought believes he was born in 1378, lived until 1484, and was buried in a secret tomb. However, he or another Christian Rosenkreuz person may have been the mythological founder of the order or simply a symbolic figurehead.

Rosicrucianism can be considered a secret society because much of its knowledge was either privately taught to a select few or hidden in coded manuscripts. However, the idea that it is a secret society hidden from public view is a modern conception. The original Rosicrucian texts do not show an aversion to sharing their knowledge and ideas with outsiders.

The Origins of Rosicrucianism

Rosicrucians trace their origins to the early 17th century. This is due to the story that a German nobleman named Christian Rosenkreuz founded the order. According to legend, his birth had been predicted, and mysterious foster parents raised him. At the age of fifteen, Rosenkreuz began his search for wisdom, traveling to Egypt, Turkey, and Syria, and while traveling, he studied with various religious groups before finally returning to Germany. Here, he gathered a few friends who shared his interest in learning about nature and science. They decided to form an "invisible brotherhood" that would continue to seek and share their knowledge with others.

In 17th century Europe, the concept of a secret society did not have the negative connotations that it does today. However, the story of Christian Rosenkreuz and his invisible brotherhood was not well known during their time. After the publication of two anonymous manifestos in 1614 and 1615, respectively, their story gained some public attention.

These documents were the Fama Fraternitatis and the Confessio Fraternitatis, which a group of anonymous Rosicrucians published. The Fama Fraternitatis sought to establish connections between the order and other historical scholars, such as Roger Bacon. It also made claims about how Rosenkreuz and his followers used alchemy to turn base metals into gold. Finally, it stated that the Rosicrucians should be viewed as a force for good in the world.

The Confessio Fraternitatis was more of an explanatory work that sought to clarify the Fama. It also said that the Rosicrucians were interested in the study of science and religion, but not magic or sorcery.

The History of Rosicrucianism

The period of 1614 to 1616 was one of the most important in Rosicrucian history. During this time, many educated Europeans received the Fama and Confessio, which had been published as pamphlets that were widely copied and distributed. These two documents sparked a lot of interest in the Rosicrucian movement. Some of this was positive, with respected individuals such as Johannes Valentinus Andreae and Robert Fludd defending the Rosicrucians and their ideas in published works. However, others thought that the movement was a threat to Christianity and society in general.

The Rosicrucians entered a period of public silence in or around 1620, possibly due to pressure from those who saw them as a threat. After this, nothing more was published for several decades, and from 1630 to about the mid-1700s, nothing was heard from the "invisible" brotherhood either. Many assumed that the group no longer existed.

This all changed in 1710 when another manifesto was written by a Rosicrucian who called himself "Sincerus Renatus" ("The True Re-Born"). This document was entitled the Witte Opkomst ("White Flower"). In it, the author stated that he represented a German Rosicrucian lodge in Amsterdam. He sought to set the record straight about the order by clarifying its history and beliefs.

The first decades of the 18th century saw increased interest in the esoteric. This led to the publication of several Rosicrucian texts, including the 1725 Fama Fraternitatis Novi ac Vera. The author of this work, one Bernard-Matthieu Willermoz, claimed to be an initiate of the "unknown superiors" who supposedly directed the Rosicrucians. He established several secret societies in France with Rosicrucian connections, including "Les Chevaliers Bienfaisants de la Cité Sainte" (The Knights Beneficent of the Holy City) and "Les Philalèthes" (The Philalethes).

In 1767, the publication of a third manifesto generated much excitement in Masonic circles. This publication was the first document to mention Freemasonry, and claimed that both Freemasonry and Rosicrucianism were descended from a common source. It also provided new details about the original Rosicrucian brotherhood in Europe.

After that, there were no more documented communications from the invisible brotherhood. However, this did not impede the proliferation of various schools of thought that incorporated Rosicrucian concepts, including Theosophy, Anthroposophy, Spiritualism, and Rosicrucian Freemasonry. In the United States, Rosicrucian ideas have been used in several influential movements, including Transcendentalism, New Thought, and the counterculture of the 1960s.

Today there are Rosicrucian organizations in many countries around the world. While there are significant differences between them, most follow some or all of the basic concepts outlined in the Fama and Confessio Fraternitatis.

The Rosicrucian Symbol

The most recognizable symbol of Rosicrucianism is a cross surmounted by a rose. This image is also known as the Rosy Cross, Rose Cross, or Rosicrucian Cross. A symbol similar to this was also found printed in the literature of several Eastern Orthodox Christian Churches. This is a reminder of the period of history when Martin Luther and his supporters split from the Roman Catholic Church. In some European cities, including Prague, these supporters were referred to as "Rosicrucians" ("Rosy Cross") because they wore the symbol prominently displayed on their attire.

https://pixabay.com/de/photos/rose-kreuz-jesus-christus-glaube-1547761/

The widely accepted explanation for this symbol comes from The Chymical Wedding of Christian Rosenkreutz, a play written by Johann Valentin Andreae. In the story, Christian Rosenkreutz visits an alchemist who uses the rose and cross to represent various stages in the transformation of matter during the alchemical process. The number three is also significant because it represents material substance *and* the three divisions of the mind (thought, action, and emotion).

The rose also symbolizes spiritual love, while the cross represents moral choices. Therefore, this symbol stands for the process of attaining perfection using both mind and heart. The structure of this symbol is reminiscent of a ladder with its horizontal beam representing the physical world. This leads to an abstract representation of a three-dimensional cross. The space between the beams represents the path that is walked during the transformation process toward a state of perfection.

The alternative explanation for this symbol was written by Ferdinand Keller, one of the founders of Anthroposophy. In his essay "Die Rose-Croix," he maintains that there was an actual Rosicrucian fraternity whose symbol was a cross with roses at its ends. While this essay is considered speculative, it pointed out that the cross with a rose can be found on ancient structures throughout Europe and Asia.

Although the Rose Cross is associated with several contemporary esoteric schools of thought (such as The Golden Dawn, Thelema, OTO, Order of the Rose Cross, etc.), each one of them offers its distinctive interpretation of the symbol.

Fama Fraternitatis

The Fama Fraternitatis presents a picture of Johann Valentin Andreae as being a restless soul who wanted to promote spiritual reformation. To give credence to his aims, he invented the story of Christian Rosenkreutz and his invisible brotherhood. His purpose was not to deceive but to pique people's curiosity and lure them into wanting more information.

The Fama is divided into four parts. The first part tells of the life and death of Christian Rosenkreutz (identified as an anonymous alchemist). It also speaks about his tomb, in which are written directions for where to find documents outlining his ideas about moral conduct. Furthermore, it provides clues on how to locate this tomb (which is said to be located in the Middle East).

The second part describes the discovery of the documents left behind by Christian Rosenkreutz. Each document supposedly had a different author, but they were all written by the same person who, in the end, was revealed to be Johann Valentin Andreae himself. The documents also speak about another secret book that Rosenkreutz supposedly authored. In another one of the documents, it is written that a sect could be formed once enough people had been exposed to these ideas.

The third part tells of a different group of individuals inspired by the writings found in the tomb of Christian Rosenkreutz. They decided to form a brotherhood that promoted the ideas outlined in these documents. And they decided to call themselves "The Fraternity of the Rose Cross."

The fourth part describes how this brotherhood ended up becoming "invisible" after a rogue faction attacked it within its midst. It also warns about the dangers of pride and greed, saying that once people fall prey to these vices, they can no longer follow the path towards perfection.

Some commentators speculate that this manifesto was intended to be a literary device in which Johann Valentin Andreae could express his ideas about how society should be transformed. However, there is also historical evidence suggesting that he did sincerely believe in the existence of an actual brotherhood called the "Fraternity of the Rose Cross."

The Fraternity of the Rose Cross

The Rose Cross is an esoteric symbol that Christian Hermeticists often used. It can also be found within the writings of high-ranking clergymen, occult philosophers, and alchemists. It is often associated with the Rosicrucians due to it appearing in two works written by Johann Valentin Andreae, in which he describes the existence of the "Fraternity of the Rose Cross." The text begins with a letter from Christian Rosenkreutz, which outlines his journey to find mystical teachings in the Middle East. He also speaks about alchemy and how it can help people transform their spiritual essence.

The longer text called "Confessio" begins with Christian Rosenkreutz being brought out of the tomb he had been hidden in for

120 years. The text describes a kind of Rosicrucian manifesto about the creation and purpose of the brotherhood. It provides instructions on how to seek out hidden knowledge issued by a fraternity of "invisible brothers" who are willing to make themselves known upon reaching a certain level of awareness.

In later centuries, many occult organizations have taken on this moniker. Some of these groups are based upon the idea that Christian Rosenkreutz was an actual historical figure who played an important role in ancient mystical teachings that are currently being kept secret from most people. These groups often emulate the ideas and practices of a historical brotherhood that was supposed to have been founded during the time of Rosenkreutz.

The Rosicrucian Order Today

The Rosicrucians today claim to be carrying on the tradition of an ancient brotherhood, which Christian Rosenkreutz originally established. This brotherhood is believed to have existed for hundreds of years and reached its peak during the seventeenth century when they decided to make themselves known to other people through a series of printed documents.

Today, it is estimated that tens of thousands of individuals consider themselves to be members of this fraternity. Not all groups are the same. Some exist in groups who practice what they call "high-degree Freemasonry," while others do not require their members to go through any initiation rituals at all.

Modern Rosicrucianism is considered a very diverse group. The secret society has always been willing to accept people from all walks of life as long as they are committed to using traditional tools and techniques. Over time, these teachings have evolved into a sophisticated system, built upon the idea that certain symbols and images contain messages that are only visible to those who understand how to read them.

Today, many Rosicrucian organizations strive to emulate the original ideas of Christian Rosenkreutz by establishing secret societies capable of preserving knowledge, self-mastery, and spiritual growth. This goal, issued in the form of an ancient principle, states,

"We are all one under the sun, a solo in luce est errare," and means, *"All are one within the universe, and only by error does he err who thinks otherwise."*

It has become the principle accepted as the guiding precept by many present-day Rosicrucian groups.

Modern Rosicrucian Organization

The Rosicrucian Order is one of the largest and most well-known organizations, which claims to originate from a secret brotherhood established during the Renaissance. The group was formed in late 1909 by Harvey Spencer Lewis, who was inspired after taking part in some public exhibitions put on by an organization known as the Hermetic Order of the Golden Dawn.

Within a few years, this society had expanded throughout North America and Europe by attracting many Masons who were also interested in studying alchemy, astrology, and other forms of mysticism. They referred to themselves as an order that is *"built on esoteric truths of the ancient past."*

Today, the Rosicrucian Order has become somewhat controversial in some circles because they have been accused of being an international order of elite mystics who are trying to influence world events. The idea is that this secret society continues to flourish, despite many claims that it was shut down centuries ago when it became apparent that its goals were too ambitious.

The Order is considered to be a very secretive group, and it has not officially confirmed the idea that thousands of individuals belong to their fraternity. Many skeptics doubt whether this society meets in person or if they simply exist as an online community. Despite these claims, the Rosicrucian Order does maintain centers throughout much of North America and Europe. A General Council governs the organization, and its headquarters are located in Rosicrucian Park in San Jose, California.

It was once believed that all of the original documents which are referenced as being published by the Rosicrucian order were lost forever. After extensively studying these publications, historians have come to believe that they are not based on old manuscripts, as they first thought. Instead, all of the literature that is used by the Rosicrucian Order seems to have been written by one individual who went by the name of Max Heindel.

The development of modern Rosicrucian groups is often seen as an outgrowth from a branch known as the Rosicrucian Fellowship. This society was established in 1909 by one of its founding members, Max Heindel. In 1910, he published a book entitled The Rosicrucian Cosmo-Conception, which claimed to contain information that had been presented to him by a group of ascended masters who lived on the astral plane. The masters believed that all of this information was too advanced for most people to understand, and they only provided it to Heindel for him to disseminate it in a form that would be accessible.

The Rosicrucian Fellowship has been accused of being an elitist group because membership requires a significant donation. Critics estimate that joining the organization costs at least $27,000-$35,000. While many individuals believe this is a legitimate price for membership, others believe it is ridiculous and overpriced because this society only provides two books and a set of lectures that can be obtained through other means. The Rosicrucian Fellowship holds its meetings in a building that they refer to as the Lodge.

In 1910, Heindel also founded a magazine titled The Rosicrucian Cosmo-Conception. This publication included extensive information about spiritual practices. It could be considered one of the first modern self-help books based on esoteric principles instead of drawing information from mainstream science. This publication was eventually renamed The Rosicrucian Forum, and it continues to be published by the Rosicrucian Fellowship.

Theosophy is a religious movement that can trace its origins back to ancient times when it was believed secret knowledge could only be communicated directly from God to his chosen prophets. Today, many modern groups claim to be affiliated with Rosicrucianism, and all of them believe that they are working toward a better world by teaching individuals how to practice self-improvement.

Rosicrucianism is a spiritual order that has its roots in the 16th century, when it was believed that this society would build a utopian world. However, it was shut down centuries ago when it became apparent that its goals were too ambitious, and individuals within the society began to lose faith in its purpose. The current modern movement of Rosicrucianism was started in the early 20th century, and it aims to educate people about spirituality and esoteric practices that can lead to a better life.

The Rosicrucian Order is closely related to the Freemasonry movement because many of its original members were believed to be involved in the craft. The Rosicrucian movement also shares ties with the Hermetic Order of the Golden Dawn, a modern occult order with many similar teachings and symbols. The Rosicrucian movement is still active today and is a private spiritual group believed to be much more open and accessible than organizations such as the Freemasons.

Chapter 2: The Story of Christian Rosenkreuz

Since Ancient Egypt, Hermetic wisdom has been sought by rulers, princes, and men from all walks of life. It is no wonder, then, that the enigmatic figure of Christian Rosenkreuz would emerge from among these men seeking to revive interest in Hermetic teachings. They are known only by the name *Christian Rosenkreuz*, which means Christian Rose Cross. Very little is known about this figure since the only sources of information about his life are the narrative accounts found in <u>The Chymical Wedding of Christian Rosenkreuz</u>, published anonymously in 1616, and the <u>Universal Reformation of the Whole Wide World</u>, published anonymously in 1618.

There is a consensus among scholars that he was probably a real person, but just as there is only speculation about his origins and travels, so too it could be said that Rosenkreuz's teachings were most likely not written by him. Given that the sources of information about Rosenkreuz were published anonymously, it is not entirely surprising that there is a certain amount of confusion about his life. This chapter will discuss the story of Christian Rosenkreuz, the society's roots in European culture and alchemy, and what his teachings may have been.

The Founder of Rosicrucianism

Rosenkreuz was the name used by Christian Rosenkreuz, a mysterious figure who is said to have lived from 1378 to 1484. Who he was and where he came from is a topic of debate since the only sources of information about his life are narrative accounts included in two books published anonymously in the early 17th century.

The Chymical Wedding of Christian Rosenkreuz, published anonymously in 1616, describes a four-day wedding in which a king and queen got married. The descriptions of the figures in this ceremony are heavily symbolic, with different characters representing different alchemical concepts. The Rosicrucian Fraternity itself is mentioned when one of the participants in the wedding ceremony asks why he has never heard anyone talk about the fraternity.

The other book is entitled <u>Universal Reformation of the Whole Wide World</u>, published anonymously in 1618. This book describes the Fraternity of the Rosy Cross and its efforts to reform the world. It also describes the travels of Christian Rosenkreuz, his pursuit of Hermetic wisdom in the Middle East, and his foundation of an esoteric school, which was named the Fraternity of the Rosy Cross.

Rosenkreuz's origins and travels are thus described in these two books. In the Chymical Wedding, he is said to have been born in 1378 and traveled to Damascus when he was 16 years old. He was initiated by a sage named Iban Amali, who gave him the name of Peregrinus. He later traveled to Fez in Morocco and then to Spain, where he was initiated by a sage named Daedalus.

It is uncertain whether Rosenkreuz's narrative in the Chymical Wedding is allegorical (for example, that the bride and groom represented different alchemical principles) or whether these books contain an actual account of his travels. There are, however, some elements that suggest the story is not entirely fictitious. For example, Rosenkreuz mentions horticulture and alchemy as two of the disciplines he studied, both of which were growing in popularity at that time.

It is also worth noting, while these accounts were published anonymously, that there is evidence indicating Martin Luther may have written them. Certainly, the writer of the Universal Reformation of the Whole Wide World spoke in a clear style that was similar to Luther's.

The main source of information about Rosenkreuz's life may have been a fictional account, but it can be assumed that he was a real person who founded the Rosicrucian Fraternity and that his teachings had a major impact on European culture. The two books that describe his life and travels were published anonymously, so not one word can be attributed to him. Furthermore, the Rosicrucian Fraternity did not have an organized structure or hierarchy, so Rosenkreuz himself did not have to adhere to any rules. However, he likely advocated an esoteric school similar to the one described in the works published under his name.

Christian Rosenkreuz's Background and Travels

Rosenkreuz was said to be of noble birth, with his life divided between contemplation and traveling. He was born in 1378 in the town of Damm in the German province of Misnia, or perhaps in Rosheim, Alsace. At 16 years old, he left Germany, traveling through France and Spain before crossing the Mediterranean to Jerusalem. In Syria, he spent some time studying with a sage named Iban Amali. He then traveled to Alexandria in Egypt, where he spent many years studying with another sage named Daedalus.

Rosenkreuz's travels and studies continued for many years, and his knowledge of science and medicine was said to be superior to that of most other doctors. According to the story, he finally returned to Germany. On his return, he joined up with three other like-minded people who shared his vision for a society of universal knowledge and brotherhood. After this, he founded the Fraternity of the Rosy Cross (Rose Cross), which became an organization of like-minded people dedicated to studying alchemy, medicine, and other sciences. According to the story of his life, as told in the Confessio Fraternitatis and the Fama Fraternitatis, Rosenkreuz died in 1484 at the age of 106.

The story of Christian Rosenkreuz has been the subject of much speculation throughout history. Some scholars have suggested that his life is a symbolic tale, while others believe it to be an accurate account. Still, others have claimed that it is a pagan fable, written to portray Christianity in a negative light. There have even been some who have suggested that the whole story is an elaborate hoax.

Whether Rosenkreuz was an actual person or not has been debated for hundreds of years. But his legacy is still felt today whether one believes he existed or not. The fact that his story has been told for centuries demonstrates the impact he or his ideas had on people. And, if nothing else, Rosenkreuz certainly helped shape European culture with his advocacy of esoteric knowledge.

Christian Rosenkreuz's Teachings and Works

Rosenkreuz was said to have brought back knowledge from the Holy Land, including knowledge about alchemy and life after death. He also studied with wise men in Alexandria, who were the inspiration behind him establishing a school of learning when he returned from his travels. He studied with various sages, who shared their esoteric wisdom with him throughout his travels.

After returning to Germany, Rosenkreuz began his work on the Fraternity of the Rosy Cross. He aimed to create a school of learning where people could come together and work toward the common goal of learning. He believed that this was a necessary step to advance mankind and bring about a better world. In his works, Rosenkreuz included quotations that emphasized the brotherhood of man and respect for all people.

Rosenkreuz's teachings were based on the idea that people can achieve a more advanced existence by studying and working toward advancement in all things. In his story, Rosenkreuz advocates that people should study and work to gain knowledge in many areas. His teachings also told of how "truth conquers all."

Rosenkreuz's story speaks to the idea of universal brotherhood and how knowledge is one way to bring people together. His teachings were very progressive for their time, advocating that knowledge is important and should be shared. Many of his ideas would play a role in developing Freemasonry in the following centuries.

Christian Rosenkreuz's Initiatory Journey to Jerusalem

Scholars have long debated the authenticity of Christian Rosenkreuz's story. In the Confessio Fraternitatis, Rosenkreuz claims he traveled to Jerusalem and then to Egypt, where he studied in Alexandria with wise men before returning home to Germany. His journey was said to be an initiatory one, in which he progresses through the grades of the Hermetic Mysteries.

https://pixabay.com/de/photos/basilika-des-heiligen-grabes-2070814/

Rosenkreuz's journey to Egypt and Jerusalem is symbolic of a spiritual journey through self-knowledge. His thesis is that truth conquers all. This includes self-knowledge, which can lead to spiritual advancement and a better understanding of the world around us. The journey to Egypt and the Middle East is symbolic of leaving one's comfort zone to progress.

Christian Rosenkreuz's Initiatory Journey to Damascus

Christian Rosenkreuz also refers to a trip to Damascus in his Confessio Fraternitatis and the Fama Fraternitatis. In this letter, he writes about spending time in the Middle East and specifically in Damascus. He refers to this as an initiatory journey as well.

While the account of such a journey is certainly fictitious, it's conceivable that Rosenkreuz was referring to a real-life excursion. It is known that Rosenkreuz traveled to the Middle East, although it is less clear whether or not he visited Damascus. Damascus and Syria were both parts of the Ottoman Empire at this time, which was under the control of the Turks. The Ottoman Empire was a center of trade and intrigue during the time that Rosenkreuz lived, which would have been conducive to his account of his travels.

In any case, Rosenkreuz's journey to Damascus again speaks of spiritual initiation and the idea that, through self-knowledge, one can achieve a higher level of understanding and knowledge. His writings speak to the idea that there is always more to learn and that we should not stop seeking knowledge.

Christian Rosenkreuz's Role in the Rosicrucian Order

According to legend, Rosenkreuz established his brotherhood in 1459 and served as its head until his death. The order's full name is often given as the "Fraternitas Rosae Crucis," and it was also known as "The Order of the Rose Cross." The brotherhood was created to foster a society of individuals who would learn from each other and advance human understanding. Rosenkreuz's role in the Rose Cross Order is symbolic of how knowledge can be used to bring people together.

Rosenkreuz wrote that he was inspired to start the order after he discovered an unnamed tomb in the desert. He believed that this tomb belonged to a great philosopher. He also claimed that he was able to obtain the philosopher's writings and translate them into German, which is how much of Rosenkreuz's teachings are usually explained.

The Rosicrucian Order was a unique group of people who sought knowledge and wisdom. It was said that its members took an oath to give up all their worldly possessions and to pursue knowledge. They had promised to apply what they learned in their studies towards helping others, both within the Order and outside it.

The Rosicrucian Order was one of the first esoteric organizations of its kind to emerge in Europe. These groups focused on the idea of seeking enlightenment and how this could be achieved. They believed this was a key point in man's development, especially during Rosenkreuz's time. He and his Order heralded a new kind of knowledge and way of thinking about the world.

Christian Rosenkreuz and the First Rosicrucian Manifesto

In addition to Christian Rosenkreuz being a key figure in the history of the Rosicrucian Order, he also has an important role in the first Rosicrucian manifesto. This document, published anonymously, talked about esotericism and the brotherhood of mystery. There has been some debate over its authorship, with some claiming that it was written by Johann Valentin Andreae, a theologian and writer of that time.

Regardless of who it was written by, this manifesto is significant because it is the first of its kind. It was a new type of document that discussed topics that had never been discussed before. It focused on these two ideas and how they related to a new kind of knowledge and a unique structure for those who sought it.

Among the works of Christian Rosenkreuz is "The Universal Reformation," which he wrote shortly before his death. It was also published anonymously, although most scholars believe Rosenkreuz himself indeed wrote it. This work discussed various aspects of society and how they could be improved, demonstrating a new kind of thinking previously unseen in Europe.

Christian Rosenkreuz's Death

Christian Rosenkreuz's death coincided with the Rosicrucian manifesto. The document discussed how Rosenkreuz knew that he was dying, which is why he chose to make this work public. He did so to provide people with the knowledge to turn them into wise men/women, such as he saw himself.

This choice is important because it illustrated the type of knowledge Rosenkreuz wanted to pass on. He poured his thoughts and ideas into this document to provide people with tools to improve their lives. His wisdom is still very much in evidence today, both by those who are members of the Rosicrucian Order and outside it.

Christian Rosenkreuz died in 1484 CE. His death is surrounded by mystery and is often only vaguely described. In his work "The Universal Reformation," he refers to himself as being ill. He also says that he does not fear his impending death but feels that it is the right time for him to pass on.

What exactly happened to Christian Rosenkreuz after he published "The Universal Reformation" remains unknown. According to some sources, his tomb was discovered in 1604 CE by a group of people who wanted to re-establish the Rosicrucian Order. The tomb was empty, and Rosenkreuz's body was never located. This is often explained by saying that he achieved immortality and transcended the boundaries of death.

The idea of searching for wisdom and knowledge can be seen in other Rosicrucian works, including the Fama Fraternitatis. This was another anonymous pamphlet, which was published in Europe not too long after the Rosicrucian manifesto. The Fama was spread around various locations through word of mouth, which allowed it to reach a large audience.

In the Fama, Rosenkreuz shared his knowledge through the character of Father C.R. He did so to provide a model for those who wished to search for knowledge and wisdom themselves. His journey reflected this and pointed people in the direction that they should take. The Fama is a prominent work of Rosicrucianism, and it still inspires people to this day.

Influences on Rosenkreuz

It is unclear exactly where the influences on Rosenkreuz come from, but there are some possibilities. Some of his ideas are similar to those found in Islamic Mysticism, which focuses on the idea that people can become wise through knowledge. The Hermetic Arts, which Rosenkreuz was very interested in, are related to Islamic Mysticism. Thus, it is likely that Rosenkreuz's ideas may have come from the Muslim world. Regardless of where his influences came from, their impact on Christian Rosenkreuz and the Rosicrucian Order cannot be ignored.

Christian Rosenkreuz was a key figure in the history of the Rosicrucian Order, and his impact can still be seen today. Many of the ideas found within the organization were first introduced by him, while others influenced his thinking. Although he wrote very little and his role in creating the Rosicrucian Order is often debated, there is no denying that Rosenkreuz was influential in the formation of the organization. His ideas are still found within Rosicrucian literature, which is why he continues to be an important figure in this society. Rosenkreuz's ideas have deeply influenced many of the books currently written by the Rosicrucian Order.

Other Rosicrucian Orders

The Rosicrucian Order expanded worldwide, with various lodges popping up in different countries. Although Christian Rosenkreuz and his ideas were influential in this expansion, other factors contributed to it. One of the influences is related to European colonialism and the desire of Europeans to explore other regions. This goal brought them into contact with various aspects of foreign cultures and influenced their views on different societies, including the Rosicrucian lodge.

Another influence on the expansion of the Rosicrucian Order can be attributed to Johann Valentin Andreae. Andreae was a prominent writer and philosopher who wrote about many topics that the people at the time were interested in, including alchemy and the Rose Cross. His works inspired people to join the Rosicrucian Order by showing them that it was a place where they could learn more about these topics. The Rosicrucians prefer to keep their structure and membership private, which makes it unclear how many members the organization has. One source states that there were about three thousand members in the 1970s, although this number may have changed since then.

As for Christian Rosenkreuz himself, he no longer appears in the literature produced by the order. The few references to him are mainly related to his role in founding the Rosicrucian Order, with little written about him after that point. This is likely because of the secretive nature of the order, which makes it difficult to discuss Rosenkreuz's life. Despite this, his impact was important enough that he continues to be a prominent figure in the Rosicrucian Order. Although he wrote very little, it is clear that his ideas influenced the organization and future generations of Rosicrucians. The ideas he introduced are still found in their literature. They will likely continue to influence future members for years to come.

The Rosicrucian Order has expanded throughout the world and continues to have a large number of members today. From its beginnings in Germany, the organization has had a history that has influenced various changes in how people view the world. The succession of its leadership and expansion can be attributed to various factors which changed the organization into what it is today.

The history of the Rosicrucian Order is a dynamic one, with many factors influencing its evolution and continuation. Christian Rosenkreuz is an extremely important figure in the history of the Rosicrucian Order, and his impact can still be seen today. Rosenkreuz's complete history is surrounded by legend. Regardless of whether the stories about his life are true, there is no denying that his impact on the Rosicrucian Order is great. In addition to establishing the lodge, he introduced many of his ideas within its teachings and influenced the literature it continues to produce. While his influence cannot be understated, many other aspects of this organization's history have helped it continue until the present day. From its inception in Germany to its expansion throughout the world, the Rosicrucian Order has a long history that is interesting to explore.

Chapter 3: The Mysteries of Hermes

The philosophy of the ancient Greeks, called Hermeticism, is one of the most elusive topics in Western history. Though modern scholars have largely ignored this tradition, it nevertheless influenced many important Western esoteric currents. The Hermetic tradition can be traced back to the Greek god of alchemy, Hermes Trismegistus (Greek for "the three times great"), who was identified with the Egyptian deity Thoth, god of wisdom and keeper of the secrets of life.

Hermes Trismegistus is featured in several ancient sources, some going back to before the Common Era. A few of these texts are considered genuinely written by followers of Hermes Trismegistus or are attributed to another ancient author who was believed to have been a Hermetic initiate. Other texts are spurious or pseudepigraphic; that means an ancient author did not write them – but they were attributed to one to enhance the text's value.

The most commonly recognized books of the Corpus Hermeticum are Asclepius, Poimandres, and The Discourse on the

Eighth and Ninth. The books record Hermes Trismegistus's teachings on topics such as God, the soul, and the material world. However, it should be noted that Hermeticism is not simply defined by what Hermes Trismegistus had to say. Hermeticism is an ancient philosophy that can be found in multiple ancient sources. While these sources are not always consistent with one another, they nevertheless have a common thread.

The core of the Hermetic tradition is its focus on understanding the nature of God, the soul, and the material world. Hermeticism is therefore based on rationalism because it argues that humanity can come to an understanding of God, the soul, and other matters through knowledge. Christian Rosenkreuz's knowledge of Hermeticism is reflected in his teachings and the symbolism of the Fraternity. While Christians eagerly look for direct connections between Freemasonry and Rosicrucianism and the Hermetic tradition, such connections are somewhat difficult to identify. This chapter, therefore, first introduces Hermeticism and then discusses the relevance of Hermetic ideas to Christian Rosenkreuz.

Hermetic Definitions

The term "Hermeticism" is derived from the name of the Greek god Hermes Trismegistus, who was identified with the Egyptian deity, Thoth, in Hellenistic and Coptic Egypt. The term "Hermetically" refers to Hermetics or teachings like those of Hermes Trismegistus.

Hermes Trismegistus was the legendary author of several ancient texts, some going back to before the Common Era. Most of what we know about Hermes Trismegistus comes from the historian and philosopher Flavius Philostratus (ca. 170-243 AD). In his work Life of Apollonius, Philostratus writes about a sage called "the Egyptian," who was believed to have lived some 1,500 years before the Common Era. The sage had an incredible knowledge of history, astronomy, and mathematics and was said to be the author of more than 36,000 books (many of them on magic and medicine). According to some sources, the sage was also an alchemist who could transmute base metals into gold.

Richard Hamer calls the sage "a figure of almost unimaginable antiquity" (The Hidden Art: Alchemical and Occult Symbolism in Art [New York: Thames and Hudson, 1981]). Although there is little evidence that points to an actual individual by the name of Hermes Trismegistus, some ancient sources did believe in his existence. One reason for the historical confusion is that "Thoth" was simply one of the Egyptian forms of Hermes, which was also known as "Hermes Trismegistus" by the Greeks.

The Corpus Hermeticum

Many of the texts attributed to Hermes Trismegistus go by the name "Corpus Hermeticum," a collection containing different works. The oldest texts are believed to have been written during the first centuries AD. However, some scholars assign even earlier dates to these writings because it is doubtful whether the authors of the Corpus Hermeticum were still living at the times when their texts were attributed to them.

The exact number of books that make up the Corpus Hermeticum is not certain. The most widely recognized books within this collection are "Poemandres," "Asclepius," and "The Discourse on the Eighth and Ninth." These three works contained almost all of what ancient commentators thought was important about Hermetic philosophy. However, there are some texts that older sources attributed to Hermes Trismegistus, but which have been lost. Among these are the "Three Books of Occult Philosophy" and "The Book of Hermes," a text that contains a list of astral spirits. Regarding this latter book, Karl Luckert writes:

"In it [Hermes] describes, in detail perhaps used by Renaissance-era conjurors and magicians, how to raise spirits from the astral plane and use them for magical purposes" (Symbols of Transformation in

the Late Antiquity: Mysteries of the Nag Hammadi Scriptures [London: State University of New York Press, 1995], 236).

The Corpus Hermeticum opens with what is arguably the most important work of Hermetic philosophy, Poemandres. The other texts in this collection are usually seen as commentaries on Poemandres. The Discourse on the Eighth and Ninth is another important text within the Corpus Hermeticum that deals with man's ascent toward God. Another key text that provides an insight into esoteric Hermeticism is Asclepius. This work claims to contain the words of a spiritual being who speaks about the mysteries of creation and the secrets of man's past and those of his future. In addition, there is also a series of hymns within the Corpus Hermeticum that are attributed to Hermes Trismegistus.

Branches of Hermeticism

After Hermes Trismegistus, the next figure of importance in the history of Western occultism is Cornelius Agrippa (1486-1535 AD). Several branches of occultism draw heavily on his writings. Agrippa's philosophy combined Christian theology with magical practices and Hermetic philosophy. His three-volume work on occult science, De Occulta Philosophia Libri Tres (Three Books of Occult Philosophy), is one of the best examples of this combination in Western occultism. The book deals with topics such as magic, alchemy, astrology, and Cabala (an ancient form of Jewish mysticism).

In the early seventeenth century, several occultist schools came into being. Among these were Rosicrucianism and Freemasonry. The Rosicrucians claimed to have a secret doctrine that contained a pearl of universal wisdom. In 1614 AD, someone from Germany sent an anonymous manuscript entitled Fama Fraternitatis (The Fame of the Brotherhood of RC). The book claimed to be about a secret brotherhood that was founded by Christian Rosenkreuz. It describes what this person had seen on his travels and gives instructions about how to become a member of this mystical order.

A year later, another treatise appeared under the name Confessio Fraternitatis (Confession of the Brotherhood of RC), which was probably written to refute some aspects of the first book. It gave further information about this secret society and its founder, Christian Rosenkreuz. In 1616 AD, a third volume appeared in Germany, entitled The Chymical Wedding of Christian Rosenkreutz (with several later editions). This volume was a fiction that had many elements in common with alchemy.

The ideas of the Rosicrucian movement spread throughout Europe. Anyone who showed an interest in esoteric disciplines had heard about this mysterious brotherhood, which claimed to possess secret knowledge related to Cabala, astrology, alchemy, and magic. Several works appeared after 1616 AD that was connected to the Rosicrucian movement. These include Chemical Pathway and The Wedding of Opposites (both 1617 AD) and Theater of Terrestrial Astronomy (1619).

At the beginning of the eighteenth century, a work entitled The Chemical Treatise or Alchemical Homilies was published anonymously in England. This was probably written by Thomas Vaughan (1621-1666 AD). He was the author of Euphrates, or The Waters of the East (published in 1650 AD), which is a work that inspired mystics for generations.

The Hermetic Order of the Golden Dawn

The works of Agrippa had a wide-ranging influence on many esoteric schools. The Hermetic Order of the Golden Dawn was one of these schools. This order was founded around 1888 AD by three Freemasons, William Wynn Westcott (1848-1925), Samuel Liddell MacGregor Mathers (1854-1918), and William Robert Woodman (1828-1891). The order's mythology was based on the legend of Christian Rosenkreuz, who was also portrayed as its founder.

The Order of the Golden Dawn is best known for its teachings about magic, which took influence from both Western and Eastern esoteric traditions. Among other things, this school taught members how to work with symbols, amulets, talismans, and the Kabbalah. These symbols were connected to a ritual magic system whose rites could be used for spiritual purification, self-knowledge, and the development of consciousness.

Membership in this order required initiation into three different grades: Neophyte (initiate), Zelator (probationer), and Philosophus (philosopher). After these three grades had been completed, members were allowed to study the Kabbalah. This was an ancient form of Jewish mysticism that was closely connected to both Hermeticism and magic.

The majority of members in this order were also Freemasons. This is understandable because Freemasonry has a tradition in Western esotericism that goes back to the Middle Ages. In Freemasonry, members adopt a system of morality based on Hermetic teachings. The influence of Freemasonry on the Golden Dawn was especially clear when it came to its use of symbols and initiation rites. Members were required to wear a specific Masonic tie to participate in meetings. The names of the different degrees in this order were also derived from Freemasonry, which gave them an alchemical significance associated with transformation.

After Mathers died, Aleister Crowley (1875-1947) became the leader for the Masonic Order (or Stella Matutina), which was a branch of this brotherhood. This order was the successor to the Golden Dawn, and Crowley developed its teachings further. He is a figure who played a major role in modern Hermeticism. Among other things, he wrote several works on magic and alchemy.

Crowley also founded another magical organization called The Argenteum Astrum (or Silver Star), which Freemasonry inspired. This order still exists today and is best known for its teachings on magic. It has several lodges in different countries worldwide, including four lodges located in New York City.

One of the most influential representatives of modern Hermeticism was Carl Gustav Jung (1875-1961). He was a Swiss psychiatrist who initially studied Freudian psychoanalysis but later became interested in subjects such as philosophy and Eastern spirituality. In particular, Jung was captivated by alchemy because of its psychological symbolism. He also compared the structure of the psyche to that of matter, which is a theme found in both Hermeticism and alchemy.

Jung is sometimes considered the father of the New Age movement because of his studies in spirituality and alternative medicine. He also had an interest in astrology, which he believed was related to alchemy. While some contemporary authors label him a mystic, Jung did not identify with this term because of its religious connotations. However, he did acknowledge that he had experienced another form of reality at the beginning of his career, which is sometimes compared to a mystical experience.

This is why Jung believed in a concept called synchronicity, which was described as "meaningful coincidences." His idea was that people are connected with the world on a deeper level than can be explained by the laws of nature. From this perspective, people and "cosmic patterns" can interact with each other even if there is no causal relationship between them.

Jung founded a psychological school called *analytical psychology*. Because of its mysticism, it has been reinterpreted as part of modern Hermeticism s. For example, Jung described his theory as an empirical science based on introspection and Buddhist teachings. In some of his works, he associated the unconscious with primordial energy called "libido," which can be related to Hermetic principles such as Prana or subtle energy from Kundalini yoga.

The Symbol of the Hermetic Traditions

The symbol of the hermetic traditions is a drawing of Hermes Trismegistus that was created by the French occultist Eliphas Levi (1810- 1875). This image depicts Hermes holding an oval scepter in his left hand. There are two serpents at the top of the drawing with their heads intertwined. The right-hand snake is often portrayed as having its tail in Hermes' hand, while the left-hand one has his mouth.

The scepter Hermes is holding represents astral light or magical energy. It can also symbolize knowledge or gnosis because it is said to have been created by the ancient Egyptian god Thoth, who was known as the god of writing, magic, and wisdom. The two serpents also represent astral light, and their heads can symbolize positive and negative energy. The left-hand serpent represents the "serpent of darkness," associated with evil in ancient Egyptian mythology.

The oval shape that Hermes is holding has a double meaning. It refers to the shape of the universe, and it is supposed to represent a "vesica piscis." This term comes from Latin and means "bladder of a fish." In medieval times, people believed this was actually what you would find in the belly of a fish after cutting it open. The vesica piscis can be used as a visual representation of the intersection between two circles, which is used as a symbol for higher planes of reality.

The drawing, by Eliphas Levi, became very popular in occult circles, and it has been used as a logo by different esoteric groups such as the Hermetic Order of the Golden Dawn or Thelema. In these settings, Hermes Trismegistus is known as the initiator of the Ancient Mysteries, who taught various esoteric doctrines to humanity. This includes alchemy or "Hermetic science," which became an important part of Hermeticism.

Hermes Trismegistus was sometimes described as a god that ruled over the ancient Egyptian civilization. However, in other instances, Hermes was described as a man who lived during the pharaonic period and who had been initiated into esoteric knowledge by the ancient Egyptians. In general, modern Hermeticism is not associated with any particular culture or religion. It has been influenced by Egyptian mythology, Greek philosophy, medieval alchemy, Renaissance magic, and 19th-century occultism.

To better understand the Hermetic tradition, it is necessary to discuss the Corpus Hermetica, which is a collection of mystical texts. This body of knowledge was attributed to Hermes Trismegistus, and it became quite popular in the Renaissance period because of its links with magic and alchemy. However, modern scholars generally agree that it had no single author and it was a collection of writings from different periods and authors. The works that are included in the Corpus Hermetica date back as far as 200 BCE, but they were probably written between the third century CE and the first half of the second century CE.

The texts that make up this body of knowledge describe Hermes Trismegistus as a wise man who was able to reveal divine truths through his writings. Some of the texts that are included in this collection include "Poimandres," which is also known as "The Vision of Hermes," and it includes the earliest Hermetic writing called the "Untitled Text." Other representative works are "Asclepius" and "The Discourse of Hermes to Tat." Some scholars also include parts of the Hermetic writings found at Nag Hammadi in this body of knowledge.

The most influential work included in the Corpus Hermetica is "Corpus Hermeticum I." This was translated into Latin by Marsalis Ficini during the Italian Renaissance, who was considered the leader of the Florentine Academy at that time. This work is considered one of the foremost examples of Renaissance thought. It includes several teachings attributed to Hermes Trismegistus. For instance, there is a discussion between Poimandres and Hermes about "the One" and its "nous," a Greek term that means "mind." Hermes also reveals the secrets of nature, creation, and human beings.

The presence of Hermetic teachings in "Corpus Hermeticum I" was influential enough to impact early modern depictions of Hermes Trismegistus. Several artists from the Renaissance period depicted him as a person wearing a turban, which is similar to how it was illustrated in Islamic art. In some cases, he has been portrayed as a sage or an angel, while other artists have depicted him holding scrolls that contain occult symbols and Hermetic teachings.

Hermeticism had a considerable impact on Renaissance magic and alchemy. For instance, alchemists used the Greek name "Hermes" as a code word for their art. They believed that his name was associated with Mercury, and they considered it to be an essential element in alchemy. Renaissance magic also borrowed several symbols from Hermetic writings and used them as part of their rituals and attempts to communicate with celestial entities.

In many cases, the Hermeticism of the Renaissance was used for political purposes. Some Italian rulers tried to legitimize their power by using occult symbols and linking them with their rule. Cosimo de Medici (1389-1464) was one of these rulers, and he became interested in Hermetic teachings due to his friendship with Ficino. Cosimo was an important patron of the Renaissance, and he also sponsored translations of Greek texts into Latin, which included Hermetic writings.

Although it is not possible to point out a single definition for Hermeticism, it can be said that this ancient tradition is associated with specific symbols, teachings, and rituals. It has influenced many occult and esoteric traditions, while its presence has also been seen in modern practices.

In summary, Hermeticism is an ancient tradition that has influenced many occult and esoteric traditions. Some of the most well-known influences it had on modern traditions include its influence on alchemy and Renaissance magic. Christian Rosenkreuz, who is the hero of the Rosicrucian Manifestos, was influenced by Hermetic teachings. He studied them during his travels, and he tried to pass some of the knowledge that he acquired onto other people. Among the knowledge he transmitted were occult teachings, which his followers believed could be used to achieve mystical goals. The Rosicrucian Manifestos also revealed several symbols which are still used today by modern Rosicrucians.

Chapter 4: Poimandres: A Gnostic Manuscript

The Hermetic writings are a collection of ancient Egyptian texts that probably originated from a priestly initiatory cult in Alexandria, Egypt, around the 2nd century CE. Only a few of the cult's documents have survived, which were found in a highly fragmentary form under the title "Hermetica" (in Greek, "of the Egyptians," hence the Egyptian provenance of these texts). Some of them were long known as "writings from the temples of Egypt" (a probable source of the name Hermes Trismegistos). A famous collection of Egyptian writings is attributed to the ancient Egyptian god, Thoth, who was also called Trismegistus (as in "Thrice Great," a typical designation for Egyptian gods). The Hermetic writings were a series of texts containing a mixture of cryptic messages about numbers and letters, as well as philosophical speculations.

https://pixabay.com/de/vectors/hieroglyphen-papyrus-alt-%C3%A4gypten-148785/

However, the combination of letters and numbers was considered to be especially important. To some extent, this belief has also influenced our culture today. For example, the Kabbalah (a Jewish form of mysticism) was strongly influenced by the teachings in the Hermetic writings, which dealt with the interpretation of the letters of the Hebrew alphabet. The combination of letters and numbers was not unique to ancient Egypt or Alexandria, although it is unclear whether the Hermetic writings have a purely Egyptian origin or whether they owe some of their ideas to Gnosticism, another religious movement that originated in Alexandria.

Nonetheless, the Hermetic writings were compiled by the Greeks. Therefore, there may be some gnostic influences on these texts. This chapter will discuss a particularly famous Hermetic text that has survived in a fragmentary form. It is called Poimandres, which means "the shepherd of men." This document is of great relevance to Hermeticism because it contains many of the themes found in other Hermetic writings.

The Poimandres

A first-hand account of the first Hermetic text, the Poimandres, was written by an unknown Greek author, who saw himself as a "prophet" inspired by "God" to write this text. For that reason, he wrote in the first person singular. He introduced himself as follows:

"I, Poimandres, the mind of absolute power ... wrote this for you..."

There are several reasons to doubt the authenticity of this text. With his reference to "God" and himself as a prophet, the writer appeared to take himself very seriously. His claim that he saw Poimandres, the "first" or "the mind," in a vision may be true to some extent. However, the claim that he wrote down what he had seen immediately afterward seems implausible. The text is not written in a singular style. Furthermore, it was written in Egypt, yet the author claimed that he saw "God" in an allegorical form. This implies that the author had a very Hellenistic (Greek) view of the world, which is strange if he supposedly wrote down what he had seen in a vision immediately. Presumably, it would take at least some time to shape the vision into a coherent text.

The above-mentioned textual problems could be due to the process of "translation." The text was written in a Semitic language, which is known as Coptic. This is the latest stage of the Egyptian language. However, the text may also contain remnants of Greek. The author's reference to himself as a "prophet" and his claim that he wrote down what he had seen immediately after having a vision would be difficult to explain if the text was written in Coptic. However, it is possible that he wrote down his vision in Greek and later translated it into the Coptic tongue.

The text of the Poimandres is divided into three sections. This division was first proposed by the English mathematician and philosopher Sir Thomas Browne (1605-1682). The book is written as an apocalyptic vision of what would happen if the teachings of Poimandres were not followed. The first section concerns itself with knowledge, whereas the second and third sections focus on ethics.

The Contents of the Poimandres

The Poimandres is written in the form of a dialogue between Poimandres and Hermes Trismegistus, who is considered to be an influential figure in Hermeticism, but our knowledge of this person is severely limited. Poimandres is the teacher within this dialogue, and Hermes Trismegistus is the pupil. Poimandres even claims to have written on stone tablets, which he wants Hermes Trismegistus to read.

The Poimandres begins with describing an apocalyptic vision in which Poimandres, who represents divine wisdom, explains the origin of the universe and how everything is composed of light. This was an important theme for Hermeticists because it explained how evil could be present in everything that exists but remain concealed.

The second section of the Poimandres is also apocalyptic. Hermes Trismegistus sees visions of future events which are reminiscent of well-known wars and plagues. This section is especially important to Hermeticists because it states that the Egyptian god Thoth will bring about a spiritual renewal in the future. However, it is not clear whether this would happen through inventions or divine intervention from another world. The second section ends with Hermes Trismegistus seeing his physical body lying dead on the ground.

Hermes Trismegistus does not experience death but continues to live in the spiritual world. He sees a "palace" and is led into it by Poimandres. There, Hermes Trismegistus experienced what he described as "martyrdom." However, his physical body remained alive and healthy. The third section of the Poimandres is a highly regarded source for Hermeticists because it deals with the question of how to achieve illumination. Poimandres explains that Hermes Trismegistus must combine his reason with faith to achieve knowledge. This combination is also explained more clearly by Nicolas-Claude Fabri de Peiresc (1580-1637), a French lawyer who was an important Hermeticist in the early 17th century.

The way to achieve illumination is also explained in the second section of the Poimandres. Hermes Trismegistus must focus his attention on spiritual matters and not be distracted by material things, according to Peiresc. This process is known as "purification." However, not all scholars agree as to the exact meaning of this term. It's also possible that the two words had distinctly different meanings. Some focused on this topic more from an ethical point of view, while others wanted purity for its own sake.

Despite this, a central theme in the Poimandres is that anyone can achieve illumination. However, the way to achieve this state is always difficult and painful because it requires an inner transformation of mind and soul. This transformation leads to a new divine self that exists in harmony with the universe and its creator, whether their god is known as Poimandres or not.

The Poimandres was probably written by a man called Aurelius Polio, who was active in the 2nd century CE. However, scholars are not certain of this attribution. Another possibility is that some parts were written by a Christian scribe and that other parts were added later on. According to various scholars, the Poimandres was influenced by Antonius Diogenes' (3rd century) book of the same name. The author of this book claimed that God was a separate entity from the material world, which means it may have been one of the earliest books in history to do so.

The Poimandres also predates another prominent work in Hermetic history: Hermes Trismegistus' teachings. According to certain scholars, this may mean that the concepts found in the Poimandres were not directly influenced by Greek philosophy when they were still spread orally. However, others disagree with this analysis and claim that the Poimandres show signs of Platonism.

The Importance of the Poimandres

The Poimandres was widely read in the early centuries CE. It influenced many Hermetic philosophers by providing them with a spiritual background for their thoughts and ideas. The author of this text claimed to have written these teachings using earlier manuscripts, which may mean that many philosophers before him were also influenced by Hermes Trismegistus.

The Poimandres is one of the most important books in Hermetic history for several reasons. Firstly, it is written in an intelligible language, unlike magical texts found throughout the 2nd century that were often written in incomprehensible ciphers. Secondly, it is one of the first and most important Hermetic texts that influenced many other scholars and philosophers.

Poimandres is also significant because it gives a name to its author: Hermes Trismegistus, which means "Hermes the Thrice-Greatest." This was not just limited to this text. According to some sources, Hermes Trismegistus was an amalgamation of several Greek people who were associated with the god Hermes.

The Poimandres focuses on ascension, which is also known as "illumination" or becoming more aware of one's self and the divine world. This means that it is not just limited to Hermeticists. Anyone who is interested in seeking enlightenment can find inspiration in this text. The Poimandres is one of the oldest books that was written specifically for Hermeticists, which means that it is a crucial resource for understanding certain elements of their history and spirituality.

The Character of Poimandres

In the Poimandres, Hermes Trismegistus is taken on a journey of self-discovery by a being called Poimandres, which means "knowledge of things." This being then guides Hermes through the universe and reveals its secrets, eventually leading him to an encounter with God or the Supreme Being. Through this experience, Hermes acquires a type of divine knowledge that allows him to understand the universe and its ultimate goal.

Like many other texts in Hermetic history, including letters supposedly written by Jesus Christ or apocryphal accounts of his life, the Poimandres is full of wisdom and moral lessons, taught through a narrative about a journey. In this case, Hermes took a personalized journey leading to understanding the universe and how everything was created.

This is also one of the first books in Hermetic history where they discuss their concept of "true" or "false" gnosis, which means knowledge. According to some scholars, this means we can read the Poimandres as an esoteric guide for self-discovery, like other Gnostic scriptures found in Eastern religions. Poimandres is not the only text in Hermetic history that discusses knowledge. In fact, this idea could be traced back to the Corpus Hermeticum, which was written between the 2nd and 4th centuries CE. This means that knowledge was one of the central concepts in Hermetic history, which likely contributed to their drive for knowledge.

The Poimandres is not only an important text because it influenced other scholars; it also highlights Hermes' journey as he seeks enlightenment and understanding. It shows how Hermes left behind his materialistic life so that he could focus on self-discovery and his connection to the divine. This is why many philosophers and scholars today still read the Poimandres, and it has impacted Hermetic history in a meaningful way that continues to inspire people.

While the Poimandres is a significant text for Hermetic history, it arguably has some Gnostic elements that can be traced back to Eastern religions. Some scholars believe that the Poimandres could have been influenced by Buddhist ideas of enlightenment and ascension through meditation. This means that Hermes may have been largely inspired by Buddhism, which also emphasizes the understanding of a supreme being and a path towards enlightenment.

The Poimandres is an important text for Hermetic history because it shows how they began to discuss gnosis or knowledge, which was likely influenced by Eastern religions like Buddhism. This means that today, we can read this manuscript as an esoteric guide that leads its readers on a path toward enlightenment.

The Pomanders, which is Latinized Greek for "the shepherd of men," or, in other words, Hermes Trismegistus, is the most famous of the Hermetic texts (Deeg & van den Broek 2). An amalgamation of several Greek cultures associated with their god Hermes (Thoth in Egyptian), Hermes Trismegistus is a combination of the Greek god Hermes and the Egyptian god Thoth. According to legend, Thoth was an intelligent being who brought writing and language to humanity at a time when everything was in chaos. As a result, a cult developed around him that sought understanding of the deeper mysteries of life through knowledge and self-empowerment.

This combination of Hermes and Thoth is most commonly depicted in the Poimandres, or "The Vision of Hermes," found in a collection of Hermetic texts called the Corpus Hermetica. This text recounts how Hermes Trismegistus is taken on a spiritual journey by Poimandres, or his "inner self" (Deeg & van den Broek 10). This journey was meant to enlighten Hermes and empower him as he gained knowledge about the universe and how everything was created, and he became closer to understanding reality.

Gnosticism and the Poimandres

The meaning of the term "gnosis" is knowledge. It was mainly popularized by Plato, who used it in his famous work, The Republic (OED). Gnostic ideas were later formed around the idea of gnosis, meaning people believed they could obtain knowledge or learn about reality through understanding and reading/observing the world around them. This knowledge, however, would often come to people through divine inspiration or illumination rather than seeing reality for what it was (OED). As a result of this philosophy, gnostic texts were not meant to be read by most people because only an "enlightened" person could fully understand their meaning (Deeg & van den Broek 11).

The Poimandres also have Gnostic elements to them. In fact, some scholars believe the term "gnosis" was coined by Hermes Trismegistus (Deeg & van den Broek 3). This means that many of the ideas associated with Gnosticism can be traced back to Hermes Trismegistus. Many parts of the text reference gnostic beliefs, such as an emphasis on meditation or knowledge that can only be obtained through self-empowerment. Hermes' goal to attain enlightenment is something that the Gnostics also emphasized.

The Poimandres have many different themes associated with them, common to gnostic texts. One of these is the emphasis on knowledge and self-empowerment. Hermes began his spiritual journey after he heard a voice that told him, *"You are immortal god"* (Deeg & van den Broek 11). After this realization, he was told by Poimandres that there is a reality beyond this physical world and that people can only understand it through understanding themselves. Hermes also learned about the seven heavens, which are considered separate realities from the physical ones. When he finally returned to his body after being enlightened, he realized that most people are not able to see what he had seen because they have not been enlightened.

Another common theme in Gnostic texts is the idea of a hostile world or demiurge. Some scholars believe that this became a central theme in many other religions after Hermes Trismegistus introduced it. In the Poimandres, the demiurge is revealed to Hermes when he asks who or what created everything. He learned that there was a "lord" of all creation called Ialdabaoth, who got lonely and decided to create other beings. Because another created this god, he was not all-knowing or powerful like his creator. However, he did not want to admit this fact. Because of his pride and unwillingness to accept that there was something greater than himself, Ialdabaoth created the world. This is similar to the concept of the demiurge in gnostic texts because it highlights how evil this world is and how people should not be willing to accept it.

Though Hermes Trismegistus was known for being a Hermetic philosopher, he also had strong ties to esotericism. The Poimandres reveal many different esoteric ideas that are still believed in today. The story of Hermes' enlightenment is also an example of esotericism. Many texts written by Hermes Trismegistus focus on knowledge and esoteric ideas. Some examples include the Kybalion, which was written around 1912, and the Corpus Hermeticum, which was written in the 2nd century CE.

Hermes Trismegistus was also known for being the author of the Emerald Tablet, which was written around 40 CE. This document has been the topic of discussion among many alchemists because it discussed many different topics related to alchemy, such as the creation of the world and the philosophy of transmutation.

Poimandres: A Gnostic Manuscript explores some of the major ideas associated with Gnosticism and Hermeticism. The text is written as a dialogue between Hermes and Poimandres, who represent knowledge or wisdom. Like many gnostic texts, it emphasizes the idea that people should seek self-enlightenment and that they can only understand reality through understanding themselves.

The Poimandres have many different influences from both Hermetic and gnostic traditions. Because Hermes was known for being the founder of Hermeticism, many people associate him with this tradition. However, Hermes was also known to have strong ties with Gnosticism, which is the main influence of the Poimandres. The text was also influenced by Egyptian mythology, which can be seen throughout the story of Hermes' enlightenment. After his enlightenment, Hermes was told that he could return to the physical world and share what he had learned if he agreed to do so. However, he was not able to return the same way because he had become wiser. Instead, Hermes had to enter the world through his son, Tat.

As is obvious from the information provided above, Hermes Trismegistus and his teachings would strongly influence many different religions and cultures. His ideas can be traced throughout history as they have been adapted to fit new purposes or changes in society. For example, the Poimandres have been used as a manifesto for Chaos Magick because it discusses different ideas relevant to this form of religious belief. In addition, the Corpus Hermeticum was a key text of Renaissance Neoplatonism because it contained ideas that people wanted to read and discover. Hermes Trismegistus starts as a pagan god, but he is also the central figure in Hermetic philosophy. His ideas have influenced many different aspects of life, which is apparent in how his story has been retold so many times.

The Poimandres has been a text of interest to many different kinds of people. This is because it contains many different religious and philosophical ideas that are still relevant to many people today. Readers often find themselves asking questions after reading the Poimandres, which can be an indication of one's own spiritual beliefs.

Chapter 5: The Mysticism of Merkavah

"All mystics speak the same language, for they come from the same country." - Louis-Claude de Saint-Martin

The mysticism of Merkavah, or the mystical tradition for chanting and praising God through the vision of His Heavenly Chariot (Ikavah), is one of the oldest mystical traditions in existence. Although there were antecedents to this tradition, such as the ancient Canaanite and Israelite Merkavah (Ikavah) literature dating back to the 5th century B.C.E., it is a mystical system that developed fully-fledged mostly during the first millennium C.E. and particularly flourished in the Middle Ages, when it was picked up and practiced by most of the Christian-European mystical orders, such as the Dionysian Artificers (founded in c. 1406), Rosicrucians (founded in 1598) and Freemasonry (founded in 1717).

The tradition of Merkavah mysticism is based on the mystical revelation of the Heavenly Merkavah (the Chariot or Throne-Chariot of God) and the "Heavenly Palaces" (Hekhalot) as described in the Rabbinic literature such as the Hekhalot and Merkavah Rabbati, and the Midrash Yelamdenu. This literature was mostly based on a body of oral traditions known in the 1st-6th centuries C.E., but which were eventually committed to writing between the 8th and 12th centuries.

The mystical practice of Merkavah is grounded in the metaphysical understanding that God is revealed in the innermost chambers (Hekhalot) of the spiritual realms. The visionary mystic would center his worship and praise of God on His Throne-Chariot (Merkavah), situated in the innermost Heavenly Palace (Hekhalot), and which contains God's Glory (Kavod). Thus, the metaphysical knowledge of the mystic is summarized in the "vision of God" on His Throne-Chariot, where He reveals Himself to be both Master (Baal) and Father (Ab), as well as Holy One (Saba).

This chapter will summarize the relevant passages in the obscure Rabbinic literature that describes the metaphysical foundation of

Merkavah mysticism. The mystical symbol of God's Throne-Chariot (Merkavah) will be explored in detail. This will be followed by a summary of the mystical practice of chanting and a step-by-step analysis of the Kabalistic Cross and the Middle Pillar, an exercise based on the spheres that correspond to the middle (or central) pillar of the Tree of Life.

Kabbalah's Origins

Many Western scholars often use the term "Kabbalah" to denote the entirety of Jewish mysticism, but the use of this term is rather problematic, as it limits the scope of Jewish mysticism to one specific school of thought. The term "Kabbalah" can be understood as an umbrella term that denotes all mystical traditions within Judaism, but it must be noted that this term is not used in its original sense by Rabbinic Jews or Kabbalists. Its origin comes from the Greek QBLH, which stands for "tradition," and this term was used to denote non-canonical Jewish texts that were not part of the Hebrew Bible.

The origin of the Kabbalah comes from certain ancient traditions that can be traced back to biblical times. The core foundations of Kabbalah are the ancient writings found in the Merkavah and Hekhalot literature, also called the "Hekhalot tradition" (b. Hagigah 12a). This mystical tradition was very popular among certain circles during Talmudic times, as we find many references to it in reliable sources such as Josephus (Heinrich 2012: 108).

The term "Merkavah" literally means the Chariot, and it is used to denote God's Throne-Chariot (Ikavah) as described in Ezekiel 1:4-28 and 10:9. Most of the apocalypses found in this literature relate to one or more of the following: the Throne-Chariot of God, angels, and ministering spirits, as well as visionary journeys to consult with deceased mystics. The earliest Hekhalot literature dates back to around 200 C.E. Some scholars even argue that it originated from as early as the Tannaic Era (i.e., during the time of the early Rabbinic Sages).

The rise of Jewish mysticism, or Hekhalot literature, during the medieval era is attributed to the rampant anti-Semitism that led to increased pogroms and persecution against Jews. This eventually provoked some mystics to move towards the esoteric, as they sought new ways to explore their religion without running into too much trouble with the Christian clergy. The Kabbalah was one of the mystical movements that developed during this period, and it continued to flourish throughout Europe until its decline in the 18th century.

The literature on Merkavah mysticism is so vast that it is not possible to give a complete overview of all its facets. However, Merkavah literature can be divided into two main categories: "Hekhalot literature" and "Merkavah mystics." It must also be noted that the term "Merkavah mystic" was first applied by the German scholar G. Scholem in his extensive studies on this field of Jewish mysticism.

While most scholars agree that Merkavah literature is a clear antecedent to Kabbalistic practices, they also admit that it is not easy to pinpoint the exact origins of Kabbalah. It is "impossible to say anything definite about the origin of kabbalistic teaching" (Scholem 1969: 202). The earliest origins of Kabbalah can be traced back to the 1st century B.C.E. when Jewish mystics were inspired by non-Jewish traditions and *"by the ancient Jewish views of God and His relation to the world"* (Scholem 1974: 3).

After decades of careful study, Gershom Scholem finally concluded that the mystical movement called Kabbalah had two main sources; Merkavah mysticism and Hekhalot literature. The latter term is an abbreviation of "Hekhalot rabbati" (the greater palaces), which is the term used to denote the sevenfold heavenly halls or palaces mentioned in Ezekiel chapters 1-2. This literature forms the core of Kabbalistic mysticism, with its focus on mystical prayer and ecstatic visions.

As already mentioned, the earliest sources of Merkavah mysticism date back to around 200 C.E., when all four Gospels were written. It is also evident that various points in Ezekiel's visions (particularly Ezek. 1; 10) inspired Jewish mystics in the centuries that followed, especially when these mystics contemplated new ways to interpret sacred scripture.

How Merkavah Flourished

The literature on Merkavah mysticism flourished during the medieval era. Some of its major works were written in Spain and Provence. Perhaps one of the most influential texts was the Sefer ha-Bahir, which was so significant for Jewish mysticism that it was believed to have been "received" by the author Nechunia ben Ha-Kanah. Scholem dates its composition to between 1150 and 1225, though he notes that it is somewhat difficult to establish an accurate date for this type of literature.

The Bahir is one of the earliest texts to talk about reincarnation, which it discusses in sections 83-85. It uses the same phrase as Ezekiel's Merkavah mysticism ('the likeness of a throne) when referring to God's throne. Another significant text was Sefer ha-Temunah, which has been dated between 1185 and 1250. This text explains the concept of "exile within God" (galut panuy Elohim) by discussing the 10 divine powers (sephirot), also known as attributes, which are mentioned throughout Ezekiel's Merkavah mysticism.

Zohar's goal is to show how the mystical interpretation of the Bible establishes a special relationship between God and man. This is done by knowing God through His 10 attributes (sephirot), which were passed down to the man at the time of Creation. It also provides

"a panorama of the whole history of the world and a description of all the events which will take place from Creation to the end of days" (Scholem 1969: 243).

Kabbalah and the Occult

After Scholem's extensive research, it is clear that there are many different types of Kabbalistic mysticism. He suggests that the various approaches found in Merkavah and Hekhalot literature are finally reduced to two main types. The first of these is quoted as:

"...the attempt to unite with God himself, which is achieved through some form of merging with him, either by being completely absorbed into his being or absorbing his divine power."

The second type, which is much more common in the Zohar and later Kabbalistic works, involves the use of meditative techniques such as "prayer, asceticism, and magic." These techniques gave rise to the Kabbalistic concept of "the ascent on high" (shelf), which is also referred to as "The Great Way" or the way of perfection.

Both approaches aim to seek God through his attributes, which serve as a means of knowing Him. But they both go beyond this by encouraging practitioners to attain an even greater knowledge of these divine attributes, which can then lead to the divulging of spiritual secrets. These secrets are thought to be so powerful that they can be passed on to others for their spiritual advancement.

Particularly interesting is the fact that Merkavah mystics often spoke in veiled language, or secret code, about what they were discussing. Many of these terms were so powerful that they could not be written down in plain text. This is because some of the early Merkavah mystics believed it would cause them harm if these secret names and phrases were exposed to the world at large.

As Scholem points out, this type of belief can also be found in the Bahir, where it is stated that:

"whoever reveals these [secrets] to his friend but does not keep them hidden will lose what he has and suffer [severe] punishment" (Scholem 1969: 252).

The Jewish mystical text known as the Zohar was written by an author believed to be called Shimon bar Yohai, who lived around the time of the destruction of the second Temple in 70 CE. The book is also known by another name, The Book of Splendour (or Radiance), and it contains many ideas from Kabbalah and Merkavah mysticism.

The Bahir and Merkavah Mysticism

Sefer ha Bahir, which is believed to have been written in the 12th century in Provence, France by Isaac the Blind, reportedly provides many important ideas about Kabbalah and Merkavah mysticism. For instance, it uses Hekhalot vocabulary when discussing the 10 sephirot and speaks of the vessels that shattered in a way that is very similar to the descriptions found in 1 Enoch of the Bible.

Both the Bahir and 1 Enoch refer to "the mystery of their breaking" (Milikowsky 2000: 110). In addition, there are other parallels between these two works, including ideas about the sephirot being *"emanations of God, intermediaries between God and Creation"* (Amzallag 2005: 402). They also seem to share the same concept of *"the mystic's quest for God"* (Amzallag 2005: 402).

In other words, both these texts contain similar mystical concepts which can be traced back to Merkavah and Hekhalot literature. This is not surprising because many scholars believe that there was a strong relationship between the authors of both works.

It has been suggested by several scholars that "the visionary and mystical Jewish Hekhalot texts have their origin in the first centuries of the Common Era" (Amzallag 2005: 401). There is also a popular belief held by many students of Kabbalistic texts that the concept of Merkavah mysticism came from the prophet Ezekiel, who is believed to have witnessed these revelations during his time in exile (Amzallag 2005: 402).

Ascetic Practices and Meditation Techniques

However, it should be mentioned that there was another form of mystical tradition that arose at this time based on ascetic practices and meditation techniques, such as fasting. This form of mysticism is sometimes referred to as introversive mysticism. On the other hand, it has been pointed out by several scholars who have studied Merkavah mysticism that there were some mystics during this time who were not strictly introversive (Amzallag 2005: 402). Instead, these mystics were often well versed in the exoteric practices of Judaism and could be described as *| both introversive and extroversive"* (Amzallag 2005: 403).

The Tree of Life

When it comes to the Tree of Life, which is one of the most important symbols in Kabbalah, there are many different variations of its structure. The standard version includes 10 sephirot on the top row and 8 lower sephirot (or paths) on the bottom row. However, some modern interpretations include more than 10 sephirot. According to Zohar, the Tree of Life is:

"the model for all that exists." It also states that "there are ten sides to the tree and thus ten aspects are corresponding to them; they comprise all the supernal forces."

The sephirot are also said to be represented by the 22 fundamental letters of the Hebrew alphabet, and each one of them has its own particular set of meanings.

It is believed that there are ten different types of angels, which correspond with the Tree of Life, and are known as the sephirot. Each one of these angels is believed to be made out of one type of spiritual matter, with each type representing a different attribute. The sephirots are also linked to the human body because it has been pointed out that the different parts of the body, such as the limbs, the organs, and the blood, all have different properties. Furthermore, there are also many similarities between these ten sephirot and alchemy because they both use the same Kabbalistic symbols and rely on a similar style of teaching.

The central sephirah is known as Keter, and it's said to be the beginning of all things. Furthermore, it contains within it all of the hidden paths and is also known as the crown. It is also believed that this sephirah contains all ten sephirot within the "primordial ether."

The Middle Pillar Exercise

When it comes to meditation, many different techniques are used. One of the most important ones is the Middle Pillar Exercise, which is a form of Kabbalistic meditation. It is believed to be one of the easiest techniques to do because of its simplicity. This technique also works on balancing energy to restore the body to full health and heal it of any illnesses.

Depending on the context, The Tree of Life symbolizes many different things. One of the most well-known examples is that it's seen as a representation of the integral parts of human anatomies, such as the brain, the ears, and even the body itself. However, it's also often used in Kabbalistic texts to represent a divine power that is known as "Shekinah."

When it comes to the Tree of Life and the Middle Pillar Exercise, it's clear to see that there is a definite connection. The Tree of Life contains 10 sephirot which are similar to those located within the structure of the Middle Pillar Exercise. It also contains 8 paths that are represented by different types of energy that flow through the body, just like in the exercise. When doing the Middle Pillar Exercise, a person is said to be connecting themselves with different parts of nature to restore their inner balance. This is clearly shown by the importance of the sephirot, which are all located within this central point.

It's also believed that the Tree of Life has outer and inner realms. The inner part is known as Atziluth, which represents the divine world, whereas the outer part is known as Assiyah, which represents the physical world. The middle pillar is located at the very center of the Tree of Life, which represents the balance that must be achieved between these two worlds.

The Middle Pillar Exercise is said to be one of the most important Kabbalistic exercises, not only because it involves the person physically, but it also involves them spiritually. It is said to be a form of meditation that allows a person to clear their mind and focus on the task at hand. Furthermore, it also works to balance all of the connections within each person's aura. This is because the energy within each one of their chakras becomes blocked when there is an imbalance in their overall spiritual health. This is why exercise is said to be so important. However, it should only be done by a trained practitioner who has been taught how to use this method properly.

Kabalistic Cross [to be performed before meditation exercise]

Stand with your feet together, arms at your side. Inhale and raise your arms out to the sides and up above your head. Say:

"Before me, Elohim,"

When they reach shoulder height, bring your arms down and across your chest in a straight line. Touch the middle finger of your right hand with the middle finger of your left hand. Say:

"Behind me, Adonai,"

At the hip height, bring your arms up above your head on the left side in a semi-circle. Touch your left middle finger with your right middle finger. Say:

"On my right hand, Elohim."

Again, when the arms are at shoulder height, bring them down and across your chest in a straight line. Touch the middle finger of your left hand with the middle finger of your right hand. Say:

"On my left hand, Adonai."

At the hip height, bring your arms up above your head on the right side in a semi-circle. Touch your right middle finger with your left middle finger. Say:

"Above me, Elohim."

Once again, as your arms reach shoulder height, bring your arms down and across your chest in a straight line. Touch the middle finger of your right hand with the middle three fingers of your left hand. Say:

"Beneath me, Adonai."

At the hip height, bring your arms up above your head on the left side in a semi-circle. Touch your left middle finger with your right three fingers. Say:

"Within me, Elohim."

At shoulder height, bring your arms down and across your chest in a straight line. Touch the middle finger of your left hand with the middle three fingers of your right hand. Say:

"Without me, Adonai."

As you touch each finger, visualize the appropriate sephirot and then, as you touch them with your middle fingers, see each one of those spheres glowing brilliantly.

The mysticism of Merkavah has its roots in the Jewish tradition of Kabbalah. When trying to learn more about this type of mysticism, specific exercises can be done to ensure they are correctly understood. The mysticism of Merkavah is deeply connected with the Tree of Life, which is the central point of the Tree. This figure is said to be what separates the upper world (Briah) from the lower world (Assiyah). Understanding the Tree of Life is central to truly understanding Merkavah mysticism.

Chapter 6: Twenty-Two Paths of Enlightenment

"These twenty-two letters, which are the foundation of all things, He arranged as upon a sphere with two hundred and thirty-one gates, and the sphere may be rotated forward or backward, whether for good or for evil; from the good comes true pleasure, from evil naught but torment."— Sepher Yetzirah

The Tree of Life is a fundamental concept in Kabbalah, the ancient Jewish tradition of mystical interpretation. It was developed by the Jewish mystics of the Middle Ages to describe their concept of the process through which God created the universe and humankind.

https://unsplash.com/photos/low-angle-photo-of-trees-
s5xNLPMxHZU

The Tree is made up of ten circles, or emanations. The first three are called the Supernal Triad and are beyond human comprehension; they are associated with God Himself. The remaining seven circles, called sephirot (singular: sephirah), represent aspects of God's interaction with creation. The sephirot are connected by twenty-two paths that are symbolized by the 22 letters of the Hebrew alphabet. A thorough understanding of these connections is essential to working with the Tree.

The Tree of Life is a system, both cosmic and mundane, describing creation's origin. It represents different divine emanations consisting of ten sephirot that are interconnected by twenty-two paths. Its origins date at least to the early centuries of the 1st millennium BCE. Students who are well versed in the mysteries of the Kabbalah use it as a guide to meditation and understanding. The sephirot are arranged in three vertical columns and a top row, with three sephirot on each column, representing the supernal realm of the divine.

Each sephirah is a divine emanation influencing the creation and corresponding to one of the ten holy numbers of the Hebrews. Also, there are twenty-two paths, of which the first is the same as the last and which represent different types of creative expression. The Tree of Life is a metaphor for the stages of creation. This chapter will give a more detailed analysis of each sephirah and the twenty-two paths while explaining their correspondences with the Hebrew letters.

Sepher Yetzirah

The Sepher Yetzirah, or "Book of Formation," is an ancient work that deals with the creation of the universe by God. It is a collection of doctrines, which was written before 70 CE, and which has been attributed to an ancient Jewish sect called the Essenes. It explains how God created the universe by combining ten sephirot, which are part of all that exists. The sephirah is part of an esoteric system that reveals the secret nature of God and creation. The twenty-two paths are the bridges between each sephirah on The Tree of Life. This is a system that can be used for contemplation and one that has been important and helpful in understanding the nature of God, the world, and humanity.

The Sepher Yetzirah names the ten sephirot as: Keter, Hokma, Binah, Hesed, Gevurah, Tiferet, Netsah, Hod, Yesod and Malkut (1). The first three are the supernal triad, the highest sephirot that are beyond comprehension. The seven lower sephirot are called the arch-angels or planetary governors and are Michael, Gabriel, Raphael, Uriel, Shabbathai, Zadkiel, and (Shemhazai). All of them were created by virtue of Keter, Hokma, and Binah. Below this triad is a second one, which is also made of three sephirot; Hesed, Gevurah, and Tiferet. These are the center of divine love and divine wisdom that correspond to the three lower sephirot.

Everything is a result of the actions of these ten sephirot, which are an extension of the divine will. As the Tree of Life is a metaphor, it reveals how God can manifest in different ways. The sephirot are also connected to the four worlds of Atzilut, Beriah, Yetzirah, and Assiyah. Each sephirah is a representation of certain characteristics and virtues.

Each stage is different in the creative process, which manifests as a human being going from the embryo in the womb to birth. Once here, they grow in stages, eventually becoming fully socialized adults in society after many years. At every stage of development, there are different needs and requirements which must be fulfilled before advancing to the next stage.

The last one in the group is Malkut or Shekhinah. It has a function in the world and represents divine mercy. Malkut means "Kingdom" and is a point of concentration at the lowest level. Certain Jewish mystics hold that it is not a sephirah but a feminine principle.

In addition, there are twenty-two paths that go from one sephirah to another, and each path is a different attribute of God. These are represented by the 22 letters of the Hebrew alphabet, which have certain meanings, connections with astrology, and special symbolic significance. The Tree of Life comprises these ten sephirot, twenty-two paths connecting them, their names, and the Hebrew alphabet.

The Tree of Life

In Kabbalistic tradition, the Tree of Life is a diagram used as a teaching tool to explain the ideas of Jewish mysticism. It consists of ten sephirot and, often, twenty-two paths that connect them. The Tree of Life is a metaphor for the stages of creation as it consists of three vertical columns that represent different parts of creation. The first column is the World of God or Emanation. It consists of ten sephirot, which represent ten types of creation. The sephirot are divine spheres that have different aspects and attributes. Also, they connect by twenty-two paths.

The Sepher Yetzirah states that God created the universe through divine spheres (sephirot) and the connecting paths (e.g., A path will connect sephirot number one with two, etc.). The Tree of Life is a metaphor for the stages of creation. The second column is Creation or Formation. It consists of ten sephirot, which are known as numbers. The third column is Nurture or Action. It consists of the six active sephirot, representing divine forces that interact with Creation and Emanation. The top row is Divine Consciousness. It consists of one sephirah that represents the divine will and purpose.

The Tree of Life is considered to be the central metaphor in the Kabbalah. It is used as a representation of God, spiritual ascent and descent, and all reality systems. The Tree of Life is based on the Sepher Yetzirah, or "Book of Formation," which explains how God created the universe through the ten sephirot, which are part of all that exists. The sephirah is part of an esoteric system, and its symbols and correspondences are used to achieve self-knowledge and understand the mystery of God.

- **First Column: Emanation**

The first column of the Tree of Life is called Emanation. It is the first creation from God and consists of three sephirot: Keter or The Crown, Hokhmah or Wisdom, and Binah or Understanding. They are known as the Supernal Sephiroth and surround the invisible point of divine light called The Monad. The Monad represents the divine will and is the invisible, unmanifest divinity.

The 22nd path between Keter and Hokhmah is called the Absolute or The Abyss. It is a point at which God cannot be comprehended. Within this column, ten sephirot represent numbers, which are part of all that exists. It is called Creation or Formation and consists of ten sephirot, which are known as numbers. This column represents the World of Formation; the first three sephirot surround The Monad.

- **Second Column: Creation**

Called Nurture or Action, the second column consists of six active sephirot, which represent divine forces that interact with Creation and Emanation. They are called the six primary directions of space; center, above, below, east, west, and north. There are also two sephirot at the top and bottom of this column called Malkuth or Kingdom and Yesod or Foundation.

The 22nd path is called The Sacred or Celestial Column. It connects the first sephirah, Keter, with the last one, Malkuth.

The second column is called Nurture or Action because it provides the forces necessary to keep Creation alive and active. This column has ten sephirot that represent numbers. They are part of all that exists and are known as the World of Action; they interact with Creation and Emanation. Within this column, six active sephirot provide divine forces to keep Creation alive and active.

- **Third Column: Nurture**

The third column is Divine Consciousness. It consists of the six active sephirot, which represent divine forces that interact with Creation and Emanation. They are called the Leaders of Attributes or crown, wisdom, beauty, victory, glory, and foundation.

The 22nd path is The Abyss or Fog, and it separates the second sephirah from the third. It represents an area of confusion between two parallel realities between which we can never find a resolution.

The third column is called Divine Consciousness because it represents the World of Attributes, which consists of six active sephirot with divine forces that interact with Creation and Emanation. There are six active sephirot within this column, possessing divine forces to keep Creation alive and active. They also provide the leaders of Attributes of Creation.

Tarot and the Tree of Life

A useful meditation is achieved through tarot cards, specifically the Major Arcana since it contains twenty-two cards that can be used as archetypal symbols interpreted in the human mind as depictions of our society. The Major Arcana consists of twenty-two cards that can be linked to the twenty-two paths of the Tree of Life. Each path is attributed to a specific Major Arcanum. Each card in the Minor Arcana is also associated with one of the twenty-two paths. The Minor Arcana consists of four suits with ten cards each for a total of forty cards.

https://pixabay.com/de/photos/tarot-karten-tarot-karten-5511610/

The Twenty-Two Major Arcanum

1. The High Priest (The Magician)

The path of The High Priest begins under the lowest point of the letter Vāv, which is associated with a path beginning in the sephirah Binah or Understanding. The path ascends to Hokhmah or Wisdom. Through the sephirah Understanding, we enter into the process of receiving divine energy to create our reality. Using the combined sephirot in this path, we can bring out inner traits that can be used in our outer reality.

2. The High Priestess

This path begins in the sephirah Binah or Understanding. The path ascends to the sephirah Chokhmah or Wisdom. Since The High Priestess is associated with the path beginning in Understanding, it also represents the first step of initiation. Initiation begins from receiving to creating our reality.

3. The Empress

This path begins under the lowest point of the letter Lamed, which is associated with the path beginning in the sephirah Chokhmah or Wisdom. The path ascends to Geburah or Severity. Using this sephirah, we can manifest a vision and bring it to reality through acts of will and courage. Since The Empress is associated with the path beginning at Wisdom, it also represents the second initiation step. Initiation begins from creating our reality into bringing outer traits to develop a personal vision.

4. The Emperor

This path begins under the lowest point of the letter Geburah or Severity. The path ascends to Tiphareth or Beauty. This sephirah is called the Sun, and it represents the sun on the Earth. Its warmth enables life to flourish. It is our Sun and gives us strength and nurtures our expression into a reality that all can see. Since The Emperor is associated with the path beginning at Severity, it also represents the third step of initiation.

5. The Hierophant (The Pope)

This path begins under the lowest point of the letter Yesod, which is associated with the path beginning in Tiphareth or Beauty. The path ascends to Netzach or Victory. This sephirah can be considered the foundation of consciousness through which we can receive knowledge gained by the sephirah Hod or Splendor. It is also related to Keter or Crown, which is above it on the Tree of Life. The Hierophant represents an authority that could provide quick access into our subconscious mind.

6. The Lovers

This path begins under the lowest point of the letter Netzach or Victory. The path ascends to Tiphareth or Beauty, which is considered the Sun and represents the Sun as seen from earth. Using this sephirah, we can manifest our visions into actuality through acts of will and courage. Netzach is associated with the element of water, which represents life-force energy that begins flowing when two come together.

7. The Chariot

This path begins under the lowest point of the letter Hod or Splendor. The path ascends to Geburah or Severity. This sephirah is called the Sun, and it represents the sun as seen from earth. Through this sephirah, we can also work visualization and bring our dreams to reality through acts of will and courage.

8. Strength

This path begins under the lowest point of the letter Hod or Splendor. The path ascends to Geburah or Severity, which is related to Netzach or Victory through Keter, which is above it on the Tree of Life. The Chariot represents our life-force energy that begins as soon as the sun of our vision is lit. Strength enables us to become invincible in front of any obstacles.

9. The Hermit

This path begins under the lowest point of the letter Yesod, which is associated with Tiphareth or Beauty. The path ascends to Hod or Splendor, which is related to Geburah or Severity employing Tiphareth or Beauty, considered the Sun and represents the sun we see from earth. Using this sephirah, we can manifest our visions through acts of will and courage.

10. Wheel of Fortune

This path begins under the lowest point of Malkuth, which is considered the Kingdom and represents our physical reality. The Sun or the Tiphareth is above it on the Tree of Life. The Wheel of Fortune represents a very important turning point in life that gives us more power to manifest our vision through acts of will and courage.

11. Justice

This path begins under the lowest point of Malkuth, which is considered the Kingdom and represents our physical reality. Through this sephirah, we can make our visions into reality through our acts of will and courage. Justice enables us to judge the past, present, and future.

12. The Hanged Man

This path begins under the lowest point of Malkuth, which is considered the Kingdom and represents our physical reality. The path ascends to Yesod or Foundation, which is associated with our subconscious mind. This sephirah is called the Moon, representing the feelings and emotions we possess when gathering information from the subconscious mind.

13. Death

The path begins under the lowest point of Hod or Splendor, which is related to Tiphareth or Beauty through Malkuth or Kingdom, which is considered the physical world. Death brings transformation to our visions by destroying old forms and creating new ones to make them come into manifestation.

14. Temperance

This path begins under the lowest point of Yesod or Foundation, which is associated with Hod or Splendor using Chesed or Mercy. This sephirah can bring our visions into our reach through similar qualities of will and courage. Temperance is the art of keeping two opposing forces in balance. We must understand it because it gives us needed courage and strength.

15. The Devil

This path begins under the lowest point of Hod or Splendor, which is related to Tiphareth or Beauty through Netzach or Victory. The Devil is associated with our desire to take the easy way out and avoid necessary hardships. This path enables us to destroy our desire for easy solutions.

16. The Tower

The path begins under the lowest point of Yesod or Foundation, which is associated with Hod or Splendor through Tiphareth or Beauty. The Tower represents a sudden loss of power and resources that usually occurs in the way of life when we are making decisions that go against our true potential.

17. The Star

This path begins under the lowest point of Tiphareth or Beauty, which is considered the Sun. The path ascends to Hod or Splendor, which is related to Tiphareth or Beauty employing Yesod or Foundation, associated with our subconscious mind.

18. The Moon

This path begins under the lowest point of Yesod or Foundation, which is associated with Hod or Splendor using Hod or Splendor. The Moon represents the subconscious mind, like a great sea teeming with life and monsters. This path enables us to take control of our subconscious mind and emotions.

19. The Sun

This path begins under the lowest point of Tiphareth or Beauty, which is likened to the sun. The path ascends to Netzach or Victory, where we become stronger to make our visions manifest. The Sun represents the intellect, like a blazing fire that lights up any darkness and ignorance.

20. Judgment

This path begins under the lowest point of Yesod or Foundation, which is associated with Hod or Splendor utilizing Tiphareth or Beauty. Judgment is associated with the Judgment of the visions we have manifested and how we deal with them, which can either aid or harm us.

21. The World

This path begins under the lowest point of Netzach or Victory, which is associated with Tiphareth or Beauty employing Hod or Splendor. The World represents the material world and our desire to make it a better place for all of humanity through our actions – enriching our lives and the lives of those around us.

22. The Fool

This path begins under the lowest point of Yesod or Foundation, which is associated with Hod or Splendor through Malkuth or Kingdom. This path is related to the zodiacal sign of Sagittarius, which means the "Fool" because it is associated with our subconscious mind. The Fool represents the power of intuition, which enables us to see our visions.

The twenty-two paths of the Tree of Life are a map found in most esoteric traditions that define the path to enlightenment. This map can be found in tarot cards, which are used as archetypal symbols interpreted in our minds as depictions of our society. The Major Arcana cards depict the path to enlightenment, which are twenty-two in number. When we consciously discover this map within ourselves, we can achieve the highest form of magical consciousness, which is known as enlightenment.

Chapter 7: Alchemy and Kabbalah

Alchemy and Kabbalah have been studied by many of the greatest minds throughout history. To understand the alchemical work and its symbolism, a basic understanding of Kabbalah is required. As a spiritual discipline, Kabbalah is closely related to Alchemy, and both have been studied in tandem by many over the years. Alchemical and Kabbalistic symbols often overlap and can easily be seen as complementary to each other. The relationship between the two disciplines is rooted in Hermetic philosophy, of which Kabbalah is also a part.

https://pixabay.com/de/photos/naturmedizin-alchemie-kr%C3%A4uter-436578/

In some ways, it is easy to distinguish between Alchemy and Kabbalah. Alchemy has a long, continuous history that continues today. It is an extensive field of knowledge with many practical applications and a strong tradition of knowledge transfer. Practical alchemy is one of the root traditions in Western chemistry and industrial technology and has its roots in the medieval world. Kabbalah, on the other hand, emerged in the Jewish community at a time when Jews were persecuted almost everywhere they lived, and Kabbalistic knowledge was shared by a trusted few. For the most part, Jews were isolated from other communities, and their mystical tradition was only written down in the thirteenth century when they began to settle in Europe.

Alchemy and Kabbalah both emerged as part of the general philosophical and scientific milieu of the Middle Ages; alchemy in the twelfth century Kabbalah in the thirteenth. With its roots in ancient Egypt and Mesopotamia (roughly modern Iraq), Alchemy reached its height of popularity in Greco-Roman Egypt. Kabbalah has its roots in early Jewish mysticism and emerged in the Middle East during the early centuries of the Common Era. This chapter will first present the core concepts of Kabbalah, both linguistically and symbolically. Then it will trace the historical relationship between alchemy and Kabbalah and suggest how alchemical symbolism can be interpreted from a Kabbalistic perspective.

The Secret Doctrine

Kabbalah is part of a long tradition that includes Jewish mysticism, the mystical side of Judaism. In its written form, Kabbalistic tradition begins with the Zohar (Splendor), a thirteenth-century book written by Moses de Leon. The Zohar is considered part of the Jewish canon and is studied earnestly by traditional Jews. However, the real author of the Zohar remains a mystery, and most modern scholars doubt Moses de Leon wrote it. The Zohar is a commentary on the Torah (the five books of Moses), and most Kabbalistic literature that followed was written in this style.

Kabbalah means "to receive," and early authorities presented their teachings as direct insights from God to early Jewish mystics. Moses de Leon claimed to have received the secrets of Kabbalah from a Spanish mystic called the Rashbi. Moses de Leon's first work, Sefer Ha-Bahir (Book of Brilliance), is considered an integral part of the canon by many Kabbalist scholars/practitioners because it contains many early concepts fully developed in the Zohar.

In Jewish tradition, many of the Torah's secrets are said to have been given to Moses on Mount Sinai along with its written text. In the thirteenth century, a Spanish Kabbalist named Bahya ben Asher wrote a major work of Kabbalah called The Book of the Pious. He argued that the inner meaning of the Torah's text is as important as its material aspect. The Kabbalist cannot simply read a verse from the Bible and understand it in its simple, literal sense. It must be studied through a process that involves meditation and insight into each letter and word. This meditative approach to learning has always been part of traditional Jewish study, but Bahya ben Asher stressed its importance. He argued that the Torah comprises 613 commandments (mitzvahs). Each commandment has a literal meaning and an inner spiritual meaning, or Kabbalah.

Early Christian scholars did not share this view of the Bible's secrets. To them, the inner meaning of the text could not be reconciled with biblical inerrancy. Although they were familiar with Jewish mysticism, they generally considered it heresy and often persecuted Kabbalist Jews. And although Christian scholars studied Greek alchemy and philosophy extensively, they saw nothing of value in what they considered "Jewish magic."

The Language of Kabbalah

According to Kabbalah, the world exists because of a rupture in God's being. This idea is expressed as a linguistic paradox in its most basic form. The only way for anything to exist outside of God is for God to create it from nothing. But if something does indeed come from nothing, then how can we say that it has existence?

To discuss this paradox, Kabbalists use several different names for God. In Hebrew, these include "Ein Sof" (Without End) and "Ain" (Nothing). Using the word "nothing" to describe God is not meant to be derogatory. It reflects a deeply spiritual concept that there is no distinction between nothingness and any other kind of existence. The term "Ein Sof" is also paradoxical since it suggests that God has neither beginning nor end.

When we say that the world was created from nothing, we use the word "nothing" as if it were a substance like water or air. This idea can be understood by analogy: Imagine a cloth. If you cut a hole in this cloth, it is still the same cloth. We can ask ourselves if anything has been added or taken away from the cloth by cutting the hole. The answer is no—the hole exists within an existing whole. The "cloth" represents God in this analogy, and "the hole" represents creation.

The word "nothing" is often used in Kabbalah to describe spiritual states of being. For example, when a person becomes spiritually elevated through prayer or any other spiritual practice, the Kabbalist might say that the person has become nothing about God. Paradoxically, elevation means becoming more fully human by removing all qualities that are not God from within us. In this sense, the person has become more real and concrete about God because he no longer has a false self, or the ego, obstructing his connection with God.

Kabbalah often uses such analogies as part of its complex language. Most people find them puzzling since they go against our normal way of thinking about the world and ourselves, but Kabbalists believe that such language is necessary to reach a true understanding of God and existence.

The Symbolism of the Tree of Life

The Tree of Life is the central symbol of Kabbalah. It can be used to represent ideas and concepts and letters and words. The Tree can be drawn similarly to a grid with ten circles in its simplest form. Some of these circles are connected by lines, while others, the Sephirot (singular: Sephirah), are not connected.

Kabbalists place particular importance on the first four Sephirot: Keter (the Crown), Chokhmah (Wisdom), Binah (Understanding), and Chesed (Mercy). These are sometimes referred to as the Four Worlds since each Sephirah represents a different level of being.

Keter is pure awareness, a state in which we become aware of God within us. Chokhmah is the flash of insight that comes to us in moments of inspiration or revelation. Binah is understanding or intellectual comprehension, and it represents God's point of view. Chesed is loving-kindness and abundance, the part of God that inspires people to act with mercy. The remaining six Sephirot represent qualities associated with each level: Gevurah (Strength), Tiferet (Beauty), Netzach (Victory), Hod (Majesty), Yesod (Foundation), and Malkuth (Kingship).

Kabbalists connect each of these attributes with the Tree's center, which represents creation. If we were to say that God is like a person, Malkuth would be the physical world and Yesod the domain of the unconscious. The Tree of Life is also important because Kabbalists use it to understand how we can transform ourselves into more spiritual beings and become one with God.

Opus Magnum

The alchemical Opus Magnum is an in-depth journey through the stages of transformation, represented by different colors. It consists of seven stages or operations; each one being associated with a spiritual state of being. The first operation is Calcination, and it represents purification. It shows that we must be purified or have our impurities removed before transforming ourselves into something more beautiful and subtle.

The second operation is Dissolution, a stage in which a solid substance is dissolved to form a liquid. In alchemy, this represents a mental and physical transformation where we can rise above the body's limitations and the ego. Separation is the third operation and symbolizes finding what is hidden or concealed within a substance and separating it from its impurities.

We reach the fourth stage, Conjunction, when we begin to transform ourselves into a new being, one that is joined with the higher order of life. We refine what we have learned from previous stages during this operation and fully understand their meaning. The fifth stage is called Fermentation, and it is compared to the miracle of bread and wine, which become a mystical substance during a religious service.

In Distillation, all impurities are removed from the substance, which has become transformed into a purer form. The final stage is called Coagulation, and it can take several forms. It represents spiritual transformation where we can transform matter into something better, just as physical food nourishes the body.

The alchemical stages of Calcination, Dissolution, Separation, Conjunction, Fermentation, Distillation, and Coagulation can also be compared to the stages of Kabbalah's spiritual path. They are not always discussed in the same order, but there is a constant return to earlier stages, so different colors often represent them. For example, the first four Sephirot are associated with the Calcination stage while Malkuth corresponds to Coagulation or Conjunction.

This alchemical process can be seen within our bodies too. Our blood circulates through the body, purifying and transforming the various substances it comes in contact with. During this purification process, impurities are removed from the organs and other parts of the body. Although we do not see it externally, we experience a transformation that eventually makes us healthier and purer inside.

The alchemists' view of the Opus Magnum (Great Work) parallels what Kabbalists describe as the process of "becoming one with God." Kabbalah and Alchemy have a great deal in common. Both traditions rely on symbols to represent ideas that cannot be described using words alone. Even though they have different origins, both traditions aim at achieving a similar goal; transforming a person and the world.

However, there are differences between Kabbalah and Alchemy. The most important difference is that alchemy deals primarily with physical matter, whereas Kabbalah is concerned with spirituality. Nevertheless, in medieval times these two subjects were studied by cultures around the world. The alchemists agreed with the Kabbalists about the importance of symbols, but they did not always agree upon what each symbol represented.

The Sacred Fire

The alchemists believed that the spirit must be released from the material elements, just as Moses lifted the serpent in the desert to free his people from physical death. The alchemists saw themselves as continuing this work of separating the pure gold of spirit from matter through their experiments with chemicals.

Since ancient times, many secret societies have performed rituals that involved raising or awakening this sacred fire, which is known as the Serpent Fire, Kundalini, or the Dragon. It is said to reside at the base of the spine within a coiled serpent. The alchemists referred to the fires of Purgatory and associated them with this physical fire that they believed was hidden in matter.

They used special substances, called quick-lime and white-fire, to help speed up the process of purification. Quick-lime is calcium oxide, which forms when you heat limestone. Alchemists use it to refer to the "heat" that helps us remove our impurities. White-fire refers to magnesium nitrate, sometimes called the spirit of nitre, which is highly combustible when combined with another substance.

Alchemists believed that the quick-lime enabled them to do their experiments because it removed all the dirt and impurities from their vessels. When quick-lime is applied to a substance, it heats up quickly and emits fumes that make it expand. This makes it a useful substance in alchemy, but if it is not used with care, the expansion can make vessels explode!

When we look at alchemical symbols, we can see what they have in common with Kabbalistic symbols. For example, alchemists used a series of pictograms that they placed in their laboratories and equipment to show which substances were inside and what their purpose was. These pictures often depicted events that were taking place at the time, and many of them refer to spiritual things.

Grounding and Centering Techniques

Grounding and centering are very useful techniques to use before performing any magical ritual. They can be used as a form of meditation or as a form of exercise to prepare your body for magical work. Raising the kundalini or awakening the serpent fire is something that has been taught in many mystery schools, including in the West.

The same thing can happen with your subconscious if you face the parts of yourself that make you uncomfortable. You can use this energy to confront your fears and learn how to become a more balanced person. Here are a couple of simple exercises that can help you do this.

Grounding Exercise 1: To Ground Is to Be Centered in the Moment

The idea behind this exercise is to bring yourself into the present moment. It is about being grounded in your surroundings which are constantly changing around you. Before performing meditation or magical work, you can use this grounding exercise since it is a good way to get into the right state of mind. However, you may find it difficult to do this exercise if you are feeling stressed or emotional.

Grounding Exercise 2: The Grounding Cord

This is a simple exercise you can use to connect yourself with the Earth. You can do it in your imagination or literally by going outside and putting a piece of string on the ground. When you go back inside, take the string with you, and keep it in a safe place until your next grounding exercise.

The visualization is as follows: Imagine yourself standing with one foot on the ground with your other leg lifted. With both hands, grab the line of string and imagine it being pulled from the ground, going up through your entire body, and sticking out of the top of your head. You can visualize a rock or some other heavy object hanging on the end of this string to bring it home. When you are ready, release your grip on the string. See it go back into the Earth and be reabsorbed by Mother Nature.

Grounding Exercise 3: A Grounding Exercise Using A Candle

This grounding exercise uses a candle flame to help you connect with your spiritual side and bring yourself into balance. You can use it to cleanse your aura and slow down the oxidation process which is going on inside your body. The exercise is as follows. Put a lit candle onto a surface and sit in front of it. Imagine a magnet sticking out of your forehead and attracting it as you stare at the flame. Float the candle in the air as if the magnet holds it. Imagine all the negative energy getting removed from your body and flying into the candle as you do this. When it is gone, you can see how your skin gains a glow, becoming more beautiful.

Advanced Middle Pillar Ritual

The Middle Pillar Ritual is a simple ritual that you can use to re-balance your energy. It helps to remove blockages in different areas of your body and helps to awaken the kundalini. When you use it with a visualization technique, you can easily increase its power because it then becomes an astral projection technique.

The ritual is performed in the following way. Firstly, you need to relax your body and try to empty your mind of all thoughts. Imagine a ball in the middle of your chest and visualize it getting bigger and bigger, filling up your entire body. When you feel fully charged, imagine that ball going into your root chakra and unleashing a wave of energy into the ground. This swirl then travels up your body, energizing all the chakras in your body. It then goes into the top of your head and down into a swirling ball that fills both your upper body and lower body. At this point, the energy passes into the earth.

You can use this ritual whenever you feel your energy is unbalanced or if you are feeling stressed out. It helps to bring yourself into the present moment, giving you the power to confront your problems.

By studying alchemy, we can get an understanding of how the alchemists saw their world. They used symbolism to represent the fire within matter and how it can be used to purify the body. By understanding this symbolism, we get a better understanding of Kabbalistic teachings, and in this chapter, we have compared a series of alchemical symbols with Kabbalistic ones to give you an insight into what these secret societies were exploring.

Chapter 8: Practical Rosicrucianism

"When the rose and the cross are united, the alchemical marriage is complete, and the drama ends. Then we wake from history and enter eternity." - Robert Anton Wilson

The Rosicrucian Order has been in existence for over four centuries, but its beliefs are not widely taught except among the more secret orders of Freemasonry. The "practical" origins of the Rosicrucians are seen in their community outreach programs through various hospitals, clinics, and institutions for those with mental illness. The Rosicrucian philosophy also theorizes that every human possesses a divine essence called the "inner god," and through meditative practices, you can not only better understand the divine but improve all aspects of life.

A Rosicrucian ritual is typically short and designed to help the participant better understand their "inner god." Through brief contemplation, certain mysteries of life are understood and practiced, such as the "mystery of the rose" and the "mystery of death." These mysteries are not necessarily unique to Rosicrucian philosophy but are concepts that have been explored by many spiritual traditions and practices. This chapter will offer an introduction to these concepts through meditation, contemplation, and other short, simple exercises.

The following are some important disclaimers to consider when practicing the exercises and rituals:

Do not perform any of these exercises/rituals if you suffer from mental illness. The reader must also stop doing any exercise if they begin to feel uncomfortable in any way. The following exercises/rituals are meant to be conducted with the guidance of an experienced Rosicrucian teacher.

Meditation on the Rose Cross Symbol to Achieve Illumination

The Rosicrucians use the rose cross symbol as an aid to meditation. When meditating on this symbol, imagine that you are looking at a flower that begins to blossom into a flower that has a stem, leaves, petals, and pistils. At the center of this plant is a cross that appears to be made of vines. Visualize the four petals on each side of the cross, having seven roses each. The cross now symbolizes resurrection. The seven roses on the cross represent the seven gifts of the Holy Spirit. These "gifts" are not considered mysterious or obscure but are considered qualities that are innate in humanity. These gifts are courage, imagination, intuition, knowledge, understanding, love, and wonder.

You can try a simple meditation on the rose cross symbol. First, sit in a comfortable seat that allows you to be both relaxed and alert. Begin breathing deeply but slowly. Imagine that you are within a rose cross, and the symbol is spinning on its axis. You can meditate on this symbol for as long as you desire. This approach aims to concentrate on your breathing, but be warned. You should only engage in activities that you feel comfortable doing.

Begin by breathing in for four counts and holding your breath for two counts. Exhale for four counts, hold your breath for two counts, and visualize a white light emerging from the crown of your head and enveloping your body. When performing this meditation, it is important to be patient and not push too hard. Simply try your best to focus and feel comfortable, and if you start to feel too uncomfortable, stop the exercise.

Meditation on Death

The Rosicrucians teach that you can truly understand death through meditation and contemplation. Many cultures throughout history have contemplated what happens after death. The Rosicrucians teach that during meditation on death, you should try to think about what you would want to be done with your dead body. You should try to imagine your own death and how those around them take the news. People commonly believe that they will go to heaven after they die, but the Rosicrucians teach that your soul is eternal and can never be destroyed.

While meditating on death, the reader may find that many difficult questions arise. Here are some common questions asked about death:

What is beyond death? What happens to our souls when we die? Where do we go when we die? Is there life after death?

While contemplating these questions, it is important to remain patient and not push too hard to find the answers. You should simply try your best to focus and feel comfortable, and again, if you feel even slightly uncomfortable, stop the exercise.

The instructions begin by suggesting that the reader considers their own death. Imagine hearing news of your own death and how you would react to it. The instructions also tell the reader to contemplate on their own soul and what happens when they die. You should imagine seeing your own body in a coffin and contemplating your next life. You can even ask yourself what you would do if you were given an opportunity to live again.

Rosicrucian philosophy teaches that it is important to contemplate death. This contemplation can be done when waking up in the morning, right before going to sleep, or at any time when you feel safe and comfortable. The meditation on death is a way of helping the reader contemplate what happens after death while also teaching them to live each day to the fullest.

During meditation, you can use various breathing techniques. For example, you can focus on slow breathing in and out in a cycle of four counts. This breathing is supposed to be done at the same pace throughout the exercise. Another technique intended to keep you calm is focusing on a white light that you envision while exhaling.

Breathing Techniques

The Rosicrucians believe that various breathing techniques can be used to calm and focus the mind. Having a calm mind is important because the mind and body are connected since your psychological state can influence your physical wellbeing. For example, breathing techniques may help lower the heart rate and blood pressure. It is also believed that breathing in certain ways helps to stimulate different parts of the brain.

1. The Fourfold Breath or Fourfold Cycle

The first breathing technique is called the fourfold breath, also known as the fourfold cycle. This technique is meant to be done slowly and evenly at the same pace throughout the exercise. It is also important to never force any type of breathing and to always breathe in and out through the nose. If you are unsure about how to perform this technique, you should consult your doctor.

For the fourfold cycle, you begin by inhaling through the nose for four counts, then exhaling for four counts, and finally inhaling again for four counts. After this cycle is complete, you should be at the point where you began. It is not necessary to count higher than four, but if you find that the breathing technique helps you stay calm and focused, you can continue to do it over a longer period of time. The reader should only use the fourfold cycle during meditation and never when feeling stressed or agitated.

2. White Light Breathing Technique

Another technique that can be used during meditation is the white light breathing technique. This technique helps the practitioner stay calm since it centers them on their breathing and encourages them to focus on the present moment rather than letting themselves get caught up in negative thinking. It is assumed that breathing in this way helps to increase energy and reduce stress.

To perform white light breathing, the reader should begin by lying down or sitting upright in a comfortable position. Take a deep breath in through the nose and imagine that you are inhaling white light. You then exhale through the mouth and see the white light traveling all around you. When beginning, you may want to focus on exhaling slowly so that it takes about four seconds to get rid of all the air in your lungs. If you find that this is too difficult, you should take smaller breaths until it becomes easier to do.

3. Lighter Breathing

The lighter breathing exercise is used to help you calm and focus your mind. It is an exercise that uses counting and movement to remain focused on the present moment. Lighter breathing is done while standing with your feet shoulder-width apart and their arms at their sides. You begin by inhaling through the nose for two counts, then exhaling for two counts. While breathing in, you should be raising your arms up to chest level, then back down to your sides again. After completing the cycle, you should be at the same point that you started at. You should continue doing lighter breathing for at least ten minutes, but if they find that it helps them stay calm and focused, they can keep doing it for longer periods.

4. Number Breath

The last breathing technique that can be used is known as the *number breath*. This exercise is meant to help quiet the mind by focusing on numbers rather than other thoughts. Any type of number can be used, but it is said that counting up to seven or higher can make someone feel anxious, so it may be best to start with one or two.

To perform the number breath technique, you should sit upright in a comfortable position with your eyes closed. Then, you should breathe in through the nose and out through the mouth for one to three counts each time. When performing the exercise, it is best to be aware of the numbers without saying them out loud. If you find that you are becoming distracted by other thoughts, you can begin to say the number in your mind, but try to concentrate on the breathing process.

The simplest method of counting is to start with one and continue to add one each time. This exercise is meant to calm you by keeping you focused on your breathing. This can be done for ten minutes or more if you feel that you need to. The most important thing is that you should not feel upset with yourself if you become distracted, but instead try to bring your mind back to the number counting.

These four breathing techniques are meant to help you reduce stress and increase your ability to remain calm. They all follow the same basic principles of focusing on breathing and not letting other thoughts enter the mind. By practicing these three or four times a day, you can start to develop a calmer and more relaxed state of mind.

White light breathing is an exercise that many people use to help themselves relax since it centers them on their breathing and encourages them to focus on the present moment. Lighter breathing is a good exercise to help the reader stay calm and focused on their body, which can be especially helpful for those who have a hard time meditating. The number breath exercise helps the reader remain focused on their breathing and not get distracted by other thoughts while also increasing their ability to remain calm. All four of these exercises are meant to help the reader reduce stress and increase their ability to stay calm by focusing on their breathing and the present moment.

Practicing Rosicrucian Rituals

Rituals can be used to help the practitioner feel calm and protected. Different types of rituals exist, such as circle casting and consecrating yourself in front of the four elements. Rosicrucian rituals are meant to be performed in the morning before starting your daily routine and at night before you go to bed. Circumstances may also dictate that the rituals be repeated throughout the day. For instance, if the person has just had their home blessed by a priest, they should do a ritual in front of the four elements so that any negative energy brought into their home will be sent back to its source. Here are some rituals that can be done when feeling emotionally or physically stressed, in front of the four elements, and consecrating yourself to the Great Work.

1. Lesser Banishing Ritual of the Pentagram

The first Rosicrucian ritual is called the Lesser Banishing Ritual of the Pentagram. It is an effective way to remove negative energy from the person's immediate surroundings and their body and persona. The ritual is meant to be done in a room or space where the practitioner feels they will not be disturbed. They should begin by standing inside a drawn circle, which will help to protect them from any negative energy they are trying to get rid of. They should then perform a scrying ritual by lighting a piece of frankincense incense and looking into the flame until they see a bright image. They should then close their eyes, put the lit incense in front of them, and focus on exhaling until they feel calm. They should then visualize breathing white light into their body through the nose before exhaling it out of the mouth.

The practitioner should then move the lit incense to their left hand and hold it close to their chest with both hands in a praying position. They should then visualize a bright pentagram painted in white light that is floating in front of them before visualizing the pentagram closing in on them like a bubble. The practitioner should then move the lit incense to their right hand and hold it close to their chest with both hands in a praying position. They should then visualize another bright pentagram painted in white light that is floating behind them before visualizing the pentagram closing in on them like a bubble.

After following these steps, the practitioner can then hold their left hand high to point upward with the palm of the hand open to the sky. They should then visualize a white pentagram painted in light above them, which will help cleanse the area of any negative energy. They should then end by holding their right hand high, pointing upwards with the palm open to the sky. They should then visualize a white pentagram painted in light below them, which will help cleanse their body and person of any negative energy.

2. Lesser Ritual of the Hexagram

The second Rosicrucian ritual is called the Lesser Ritual of the Hexagram. It is best for this type of ritual if there are four people present, one representing each element. All four people must be in good health and feel comfortable performing the ritual together. They can begin by lighting a white candle in front of each element represented in the ritual. They should then stand in the center of an equal-armed cross, with their arms in a praying position and their fingers touching in the middle. The cross represents balance and is where all four elements meet. They should then do the Lesser Banishing Ritual of the Pentagram while visualizing a bright white pentagram painted in light above and below them. Once they have done the banishing ritual, they should begin to visualize a bright white hexagram painted in light, forming an invisible barrier around them. They should then visualize a bright white pentagram painted in light above them and below them, which will help cleanse the area of any negative energy. They should then visualize a bright white hexagram painted in light inside of them that will help to keep the body healthy.

3. Rose Cross Ritual

The third Rosicrucian ritual is called the Rose Cross Ritual. This ritual aims to create an imaginary wall of protection and cleansing that can fortify our consciousness beyond the material world. It is best to do this ritual late at night in order to clear your mind of thoughts and distractions before going to sleep. The practitioner should begin by lying down in a comfortable position on their back. They should then visualize a bright white light descending from the sky and filling up their head with sacred energy. They should then visualize themselves swimming in a beautiful ocean that is filled with white light and positive energy. The practitioner should then visualize a bright white rose with 14 white petals forming out of the water and going all the way up to their head. They should then visualize a bright gold cross descending from the sky and going straight through the middle of the rose.

When they hold their right hand up high, they should visualize a bright white pentagram painted in light above them, which will help cleanse the area of any negative energy. When they hold their left hand up high, they should visualize a bright white pentagram painted in light below them, which will help cleanse their body and person of any negative energy.

These three rituals are meant to bring positive change and cleansing into your life. The Lesser Banishing Ritual of the Pentagram is a ritual meant to cleanse your living space and person. The Lesser Ritual of the Hexagram is meant to balance the energy of all elements within ourselves. The Rose Cross Ritual is meant to help create an imaginary wall of protection and cleansing.

These three rituals are all meant to cleanse yourself on a spiritual level. The purpose of cleansing yourself is so you can achieve enlightenment and be closer to God. In Kabala, the Hebrew term for God is Ein Sof, which means that nothing can exist or live outside of God. This is because words cannot describe the magnificence of God, so everything that exists is an extension of God and lives within Him. Therefore, everything that exists is God and God is everything that exists.

Rosicrucianism is a form of modern-day mysticism based on Christian Kabala and Hermeticism. It was founded by the German doctor and occultist Christian Rosenkreuz in the early 15th century. Rosicrucianism based its teachings on the study of Christian Kabala and Hermeticism. Kabala is a form of Jewish mysticism that was influenced by the Qur'an, Hinduism, and the Hebrew text, Sefer Yetzirah. Hermeticism is a system of thought influenced by the ancient Greco-Roman world's scientific and philosophical traditions.

Chapter 9: The Daily Mystic

"I will meditate on your precepts and fix my eyes on your ways." (Psalm 119:15).

The study and practice of the Rosicrucian mystical elements can bring you much closer to God than you may think. Meditation, grounding, shielding, prayer, and ritual are all vital tools in the mystic's arsenal. Rosicrucian philosophy gives insights to enlighten us in these endeavors. Daily meditation is the most important of all the mystical practices. It teaches us to avoid getting lost in our world and prevents us from being a slave to our thoughts. Grounding and shielding are great protection in our psychic battles. Prayer binds us to God and allows us to speak with Him directly. After meditation, prayer is the most important and vital tool in the mystic artist's arsenal. Ritual helps us structure our day and give meaning to each moment. This chapter will detail some of these mystical arts and how they help us on our path to God.

https://pixabay.com/de/photos/yoga-frau-see-drau%C3%9Fen-lotus-pose-2176668/

Meditation for Rosicrucian Mystics

The Rosicrucian philosophy is built on the foundation of meditation. This is the heart and soul of Rosicrucian mysticism. Meditation is a spiritual exercise that teaches us to become masters of our thoughts. It is the center from which all other arts and sciences are comprehended. Meditation is the entrance into mystical thinking and being, from which we can escape from our mundane lives and enter a world of infinite possibility.

The Rosicrucian daily prayer segues into meditation. Meditation is a spiritual tool that helps us keep a balance in our lives. It teaches us how to let go of the world and enter a trance-like state. It is a practical tool to help us avoid being held captive by our thoughts. Meditation is the time when we withdraw from our normal lives and enter into a new world that lies within us. It brings both time and space to a standstill, allowing us to contemplate life's great mysteries. Meditation is a two-way street providing tremendous advantages both internally and externally. It is meant to bring us closer to God.

Meditation is the key that opens the door to many other mystical avenues, including grounding, shielding, and prayer. Meditation is the heart of Rosicrucian magic and mysticism. It can help us withdraw from this world of illusions and build our inner strength. Meditation makes us strong enough to stand on our own two feet but still encourages us to look up at the stars.

Meditation is a wonderful exercise that mystics, saints, and sages have used throughout the centuries to achieve higher states of consciousness. Many people let their minds run wild with never-ending thoughts. These endless thoughts can become a heavy burden and lead to mental illness, depression, and even suicide. Meditation teaches us how to bring order into our thinking. This Rosicrucian tool helps us change a chaotic mind into a contemplative one. This is the only way we can see clearly and think rationally in our modern age. Meditation has been used for centuries to achieve the ultimate goal of mysticism, the union with God.

Grounding

Grounding is an important piece of the Rosicrucian tool kit. Grounding is a method of psychic protection. It comes into play when having to deal with a psychic attack, curses, black magic, and the like. Grounding protects our auric field by whipping up a protective layer covering our astral body. It is not a subtle tool, but it is an effective one. The practice of grounding can help you find your center in this world. On a physical level, when we are grounded, it means our feet are firmly planted on the ground. This is how it works on an astral level as well. When our feet are firmly planted, we are not swayed by the storms of life. Grounding helps us to develop the willpower necessary to succeed in this world. It can help you focus on your goals.

Grounding forces you to bring your mind back into the here and now. This is essential for survival in today's materialistic world. The practice of grounding helps us find our way in the world. It teaches us not to be dependent on anyone but ourselves. This can help us achieve great things in our lives. The idea of grounding is to walk barefoot outdoors and let the earth's energies flow through us, helping us relieve stress and recharge our batteries.

When your auric field is open, you are more receptive to energies of both the good and bad sort. Suppose you do not pay attention to your energy. In that case, you can become a channel for negative energies that bring misfortune into your life. Negative entities can use your auric field to access this world. They can even take control of your physical body and cause havoc here below. Grounding helps keep your auric field closed, protecting you from "bad vibes."

Shields

When the dangers of life threaten us, shields are put up to protect ourselves. They can become an impenetrable wall, blocking any negative energy whatsoever. Shields are a constant psychic barrier that remains in place around you at all times. They can be seen as an invisible energy field that keeps us safe from harm.

Grounding and shielding go hand in hand, with grounding giving us the strength we need to empower our shields. This is why we need both grounding and shielding for maximum protection! A shield is a wall that wards off negative energies. It can bounce back any negative energy directed at you before it reaches its target. This is a skill that needs practice to be mastered. Some psychic attacks are very strong and take a lot of strength to ward off. Negative entities cannot break through well-developed shields.

Shields can be as strong as diamonds, keeping away bad vibes of any sort. They shield us from the psychic vampires out there who want to suck our energy and make us weak. They block out any psychic attack and the like, keeping our auric field closed to negative energies. Our shields do not allow any negative energies to penetrate them. They can be a psychic shield that works like a mirror, reflecting any negative energy back to its sender.

Shields can be a wall that keeps us safe from the danger of the outside world. They are not barriers but rather metaphysical walls that keep negativity from getting to us. The strength of your shield depends on how much psychic energy you put into its construction. Shields come in different colors and shapes, depending on the nature of the energy you want to shield. As you develop your psychic abilities, you can fine-tune your shields and make them even more effective. Like anything else in esoteric practice, shields take practice and patience to master.

Daily Practice for Protection

The best insurance against black magic is to practice grounding and shielding daily. Visualize your protective white light surrounding you like a cloak at all times. The more often you practice this, the better you will become. You can also surround yourself with divine white fire whenever you require protection if you don't feel comfortable working with your energy.

You can also call on Archangel Michael for protection. He is the one we go to when we need protection of any sort, and he is the leader of the angels. He is responsible for keeping order in heaven and preventing any catastrophes from happening here below. The archangels are the ones who are responsible for protecting our planet from negative energies.

The daily practice of being grounded will keep your shield in place. No matter what job or task you are doing, when you ground, always remember to do the grounding exercise before going about your business. You never know when negative energy might try to get inside your auric field and cause some mischief.

Prayers and Mantras

Prayer is one of the best ways to keep your shield in place. Prayer can help create a spiritual connection between you and God. As you pray, visualize your shield around you. Praying helps to strengthen the connection between you and your higher self. It also strengthens your connection with the angels.

Prayer works best when you take a few minutes every morning to sit quietly and recite it out loud. You can pray for protection or use any prayer you like, and Mantras are also good for keeping your shield in place. As always, be careful not to overdo it, as anything that is done excessively can be harmful.

Anyone who practices magic should reflect on what he is doing before he does it and always keep safety in mind. Taking the time to think about what you are doing will help to keep you safe from any accidents that might arise if your mind wanders off elsewhere. Don't neglect visualization when working with any magickal tools. Visualization is very important when dealing with energy, and it helps to keep everything in your auric field under control. The more you practice this, the better you will become.

Night-Time Visualization

The act of visualization is very important for keeping your auric field safe and sound. If you visualize your energy following the proper path inward and outward, you will have much more control over it. The moment you visualize your energy moving in this fashion, negative energies are unable to penetrate your auric field. The only people capable of breaking through your auric field are those who can see it. However, those who can see auras will not be able to read your thoughts. The only way they will be able to see your aura is if you are projecting it. If you are grounded and aware of your auric field, you are in total control of it at all times.

To practice this nightly visualization, sit down and relax. Close your eyes and take several deep breaths before beginning the exercise. When you are ready, visualize the events of your day, starting with the events of the evening and working backward to all the events that transpired in the morning. This technique is especially effective for those who have a difficult time recalling things from the past. In addition to keeping you grounded, this nightly exercise will also help you to stay on track throughout the day.

Do this magical exercise for a month, and your shield will be in place. You will then be ready to work with any sort of magick that you want to work with, including your daily meditation. Keep in mind that anything done excessively can be harmful, so don't forget to give your auric field a break every once in a while. This exercise helps to put you back into harmony with yourself. It also teaches you how to control your thoughts and actions.

All of these exercises will help you to stay in tune with who you are throughout the day and will give you more insight into the Law of Cause and Effect.

The Law of Cause and Effect

It is a good idea to be aware of the Law of Cause and Effect when working with any magickal tools. Any spells or rituals that are performed will come back to you three-fold. This means that any spell you cast will come back to you three times stronger than it was when you sent it out. If, for some reason, you do not want the outcome of a spell to occur, do not cast the spell in the first place. The same goes for everything else we do throughout our day, including our thoughts and actions. Everything we do will come back to us three-fold, so we must be mindful o before we act or speak. Your actions can affect the way people view you and view your message.

There are plenty of tools that you can use in your quest for spiritual growth. There is no need to stick with one tool or another, but you must be aware of the implications of everything you do. It's important to take some time out daily to practice grounding and visualization. If you experience any problems, contact a local metaphysical store for assistance, or do your research online. The tools listed in this chapter are all safe to use and will benefit you in one way or another. It is up to you to choose the path that best suits your needs and will allow you to grow spiritually.

Bonus I: The Secret Signs of the Rosicrucians

The Secret Signs of the Rosicrucians originated with a medical doctor and occultist, Franz Hartmann, who drew upon The Universal White Brotherhood, a loosely organized occult society with branches in Europe, America, Asia, and Australia, for their teachings. Hartmann incorporated the sixteen Secret Signs of the Rosicrucians in his book, The Life Beyond Death, first published in 1896. His writings brought the Secret Signs to light for the first time; previously, they were only passed down orally from member to member in the Universal White Brotherhood. This chapter will discuss each of the Secret Signs.

The Sixteen Secret Signs of the Rosicrucians

1. The Sign of Patience

This sign indicates that the adept is ready to wait for eons for the Divine Plan to unfold. And they are willing to be patient with themselves, others, and the process of life. The Sign of Patience is a call for peace, acceptance, and objectivity. It is used in the presence of someone who may be overly emotional to remind them to exercise patience and tolerance.

By using this sign, the adept shows that they are serenely detached from the outcome.

2. The Sign of Kindness or Charity

The Sign of Kindness or Charity is an appeal for peace. This sign calls on the adepts to show kindness, sympathy, empathy, and benevolence to others. It also relates to the Rosicrucian doctrine that we should be gentle with ourselves and develop patience with our shortcomings. When the Sign of Kindness or Charity is used in public, it emphasizes that we should be compassionate and gentle, even with those who are hostile to us.

3. The Sign of Envying

The Sign of Envying is used when the Rosicrucian adept wishes to discourage envy or to call for gratitude. It appeals for self-awareness, self-regulation, and release from the emotional vulnerability associated with envy. This sign helps cultivate gratitude in the adept's life while discouraging feelings of discontent caused by coveting what others have. The Rosicrucian adept uses this sign when they are tempted to become envious.

4. The Sign of Lying

By using the Sign of Lying, the adept is calling for honesty and integrity in their lives. It is a reminder to be truthful with themselves and others. This sign can also come into play when someone feels they have been lied to or when they wish to lie in order to help themselves or someone else. The Sign of Lying can also be used when a group member feels the need to break a pact or promise.

5. The Sign of Covetousness

The Sign of Covetousness is an appeal for compassion and understanding. It is used to help the adept overcome their greed, materialism, and self-centered nature by encouraging contentment with what they have. By asking for a change of perspective, this sign develops your sense of compassion and awareness. It is used when you feel that you have been or are being deprived of something that you want.

6. The Sign of Wrath

When you feel enraged, this sign calls for self-control. It reminds you to refrain from violence and instead cultivate peace within yourself. This sign can also be used in situations where anger or violence is directed at you. The Sign of Wrath helps develop patience and self-regulation in your life and encourages nonviolence as a way of life.

7. The Sign of Boastfulness

By using the Sign of Boastfulness, you call on your higher mind to help you to overcome your pride and boastfulness. It is an appeal for humility, and it helps you to be grateful for your talents and abilities without needing to boast or brag. The Sign of Boastfulness reminds you about being humble, even when you have done or experienced great things.

8. The Sign of Arrogance

The Sign of Arrogance is used to help you to overcome your sense of superiority and call on the higher mind to be humbler. It calls for self-awareness, self-honesty, and self-regulation. The Rosicrucian adept uses this sign when they feel that they are better, smarter, or more capable than other people.

9. The Sign of Ambition

This sign is used to represent the Rosicrucian doctrine that we should aim high but not allow ourselves to be consumed by our ambitions. It encourages us to set our goals high but work with diligence and perseverance to achieve them. It also promotes self-discipline and is used when you feel overwhelmed by your ambition. The Rosicrucian adept uses this sign when they feel the need to lower their expectations or work more patiently and carefully toward achieving their goals.

10. The Sign of Justice

The Rosicrucian doctrine of Justice is a reminder to be fair and impartial to all people, even when we feel wronged or hurt by them. It is used to call on the higher mind for assistance with balance, self-control, or detachment. This sign teaches us that by being fair and just, we will be able to rise above our grievances. It is used when the adept feels that they are being treated unfairly or when they feel offended by something another person has said or done.

11. The Sign of Purity

The Rosicrucian doctrine of Purity reminds the adept at exercising moderation in all things, including speech, food, sexual expression, pleasure, and entertainment. It is used to develop control over the senses and help the user to avoid debauchery, addiction, or gluttony. This sign is also used to help you overcome your sense of guilt or shame. The sign encourages you to accept yourself as you are, without needing to feel guilty for past mistakes and experiences.

12. The Sign of Faith

This sign is used in the presence of someone who may not appear religious or spiritual to convey that they are part of the spiritual hierarchy. It is used to awaken faith, hope, and trust in others. The Sign of Faith also symbolizes that God's wisdom can be accessed at any time and that the guidance of the spirit guides is always available. This sign is a reminder to open up one's mind and heart and not let fear or doubt interfere with the process of listening.

13. The Sign of Love

This sign is used to convey an atmosphere of love and harmony. It can also be used to help others feel more peaceful and relaxed or to help them remember that we are all members of the human race. This sign can be used when we feel angry with someone to help the other person understand that we are not trying to hurt them but simply want them to feel more love. The sign calls on the higher mind to help us overcome our anger and sense of dislike toward them.

14. The Sign of Union

The sign of Union is used as a reminder that we are all one and that the Universe is an expression of singular unity. It also represents God's promise to bring us together in a deeper understanding of the truth. This sign is used to help dissolve conflicts and promote harmony, especially when it is difficult to unite our feelings with someone else's. It calls on the higher mind to help us find this greater truth and unify our experiences with another person in love and understanding.

15. The Sign of Labor

The sign of Labor represents the Rosicrucian teaching that we should work diligently to achieve our goals. It also represents the principle of Karma and reminds us that we must be careful with what we create, as it will return to us. This sign is used to help focus the energy of our thoughts, words, and actions. It helps us remain humble through our hard work. The sign reminds us that every idea, thought, and word carried out in action is magnified tenfold. It also reminds us to always be grateful for the gifts that we have been given.

16. The Sign of Self-Sacrifice

People use this sign to remind themselves that they need to be willing to give up their attachments in order for spiritual growth to occur. This sign is used to call on the higher self for discernment while discarding what is not of value and developing a deeper connection with the spiritual self. When used in conjunction with the signs of Union, it helps us to understand that by giving of ourselves, we have more to share with others.

The sixteen secret signs that medical doctor and occultist Franz Hartmann created for the Fraternity of the Rosy Cross encourage us to live a life full of love, faith, hope, and understanding. The signs remind us that there are indeed spiritual guides who are always available to help us. They also encourage us to give of ourselves to gain the greatest rewards, including spiritual enlightenment and higher understanding. By practicing the secret signs of the Rosicrucians, we can better ourselves and help others.

Bonus II: Becoming Rosicrucian

To become a Rosicrucian, you must first be a truly honest seeker of knowledge and wisdom. You must have developed a discerning mind that does not stray to the left or right but seeks truth for its own sake. You must be willing to go wherever the search may take you and have a willingness to sacrifice preconceived notions or personal desires for truth. You must also be willing to put in the work necessary to make yourself worthy of the Order.

https://unsplash.com/photos/framed-eyeglasses-on-top-open-book-ABAmxzlot8E

As students study various aspects of Nature, particularly that which has gone unnoticed or unexplored by modern science, they will begin to realize that there are many secrets yet to be revealed. There are forces at work in the world around us, sometimes visible and sometimes not that work in ways that are not always obvious. Those with open minds and hearts will realize there is more to the world than meets the eye, and those who cannot recognize this must either be blind, deaf, and dumb or else willfully ignorant.

Many paths lead to the Temple of Wisdom, but there is only one Temple. The wise student will not allow themselves to be distracted by schools or organizations that appear to offer more than they can deliver. They will keep their eyes on the goal and follow those signs which show them the way. This chapter has been written to provide a brief introduction for those who might wish to pursue further studies.

The Steps to Initiation

There are five steps to becoming a Rosicrucian that must be pursued in order. These are the Probationer, Neophyte, Zelator, Theoricus, and Practicus. There is an optional sixth step called the Portal. In all regular Masonic and Rosicrucian organizations, a period of probation precedes all higher degrees. The goal is the same for both, and this is to determine if the candidate has the necessary qualities to be admitted to the group.

The Probationer Degree

Every regular Masonic and Rosicrucian order is made up of three degrees, sometimes called the Blue Lodge, because, in olden times, the room where such meetings were held was decorated with blue cloth. The first degree is called the Entered Apprentice, or more commonly, just the First Degree. The second degree adds a few lessons to the first, and it is called the Fellow Craft Degree. The third degree, which is sometimes referred to as *Master Mason Degree*, adds still more lessons to those who have learned the knowledge of the first two degrees. While the first two degrees generally only require some memorization and theatrical presentations, the third degree usually requires some physical work such as climbing ladders or crawling through small spaces.

The Zelator Degree

The second degree is called the Zelator Degree. In certain organizations, this is often referred to as the "Introduction to Alchemy" or some similar title. Besides having more lessons and symbolic plays than the first degree, there is a requirement to memorize the elemental table of the Middle Pillar along with certain signs, grips, passwords, and other information. While the first degree is fairly simple to obtain, the knowledge of how to pass the tests for the second degree is generally reserved for those who have proven themselves.

The Neophyte Degree

As the candidate passes through the testing period, they are often given some basic knowledge to prepare them for the next degree. This is called the Neophyte Degree, or sometimes just "the Initiation," and it requires only a few weeks or months of study. It generally rests on one's understanding of Sun worship, alchemy, numerology, astrology, and other similar subjects.

A common tradition in Masonic groups is for the new candidate to choose a name by which they will be known in this degree. Often, they select their own in some way that reveals something about their personality and background. In this way, they announce their intentions as clearly as possible and show that they have at least some understanding of those arts which are so highly prized by Rosicrucians.

The Theoricus Degree

In most Masonic and Rosicrucian organizations, the next step is called the Theoricus Degree. It will give a person a deeper insight into metaphysics and alchemy as well as help build their character so they can learn to distinguish between right and wrong. The equivalent degree in Freemasonry is called the "Fellow Craft" or Second Degree. In Rosicrucian orders, it is usually called the "Practicus" Degree. This degree often includes lectures on such topics as the seven principles of alchemy and how they relate to one's psychic development, the uses of Sun worship, and what qualities a Rosicrucian should strive for in their daily lives.

The Practicus or Portal Degree

The final step to becoming a Rosicrucian is called the Portal Degree, or in Freemasonry, it is often referred to as the "Master Mason" degree. It adds more knowledge about astrology, alchemy, and other metaphysical ideas that help learn how to improve one's mental abilities. This stage of instruction brings together all that the candidate has learned up to this point, and they are given tools that will help them accomplish their ultimate goal of bringing order out of chaos. This degree often includes a series of lectures on the subjects of medicine, theosophy, and related disciplines.

The Preparation

In addition to the degree ceremonies, there are other requirements for becoming a Rosicrucian. It is very common for members of the Order to have an interest in many different areas of study. This allows them to gain a well-rounded perspective on the world and also helps them become familiar with a wider range of topics. In Rosicrucian Orders, it is often expected that the new member has a good understanding of these topics before they are allowed to join:

- **Astrology:** They should be familiar with the position of the Sun, Moon, and planets in the zodiac at the time of their birth.

- **Alchemy:** They should display an understanding of what alchemy is and how it relates to the Three Great Principles of Hermes Trismegistus. In addition, they should be able to do basic alchemical experiments and understand some of the basic symbolism found in alchemical imagery.

- **Magic:** The new member should have a general idea of what magic is and how it relates to other metaphysical ideas. If they are unsure, the Order may allow them to study relevant topics for a few months before they are accepted as a member.

- **Religious Studies:** They should be familiar with the basic stories and principles of several different religions. If they are still unsure, Rosicrucian groups may allow them to study Christianity and a few other religions for a short time before they are initiated.

Official Groups

Many different Rosicrucian groups have chapters in various parts of the world. Some of them are small, while others have many different chapters. These groups often have websites that are listed on the Rosicrucian Order website. These groups are all under the auspices of one of the many different recognized orders within Rosicrucianism. Some of the most well-known Rosicrucian Orders include:

- The Ancient and Mystical Order Rosae Crucis, or AMORC

- Societas Rosicruciana in America

- The Martinist Order

- Fraternitas Rosae Crucis, or FRC

- The Hermetic Order of the Golden Dawn

- The Builders of the Adytum, or BOTA

Resources

If you are interested in joining a Rosicrucian order, there are several good resources that you can use to find out more information about them.

- The Rosicrucian FAQ provides detailed information about how to join most Rosicrucian groups.

- The Official website of the Rosicrucian Order provides information about how to join AMORC.

- The Societas Rosicruciana in America website has information about how to join their group.

- The Martinist Order website has information about how to join their group, including a form that can be downloaded and sent in to begin the membership process.

- The FRC website has lots of information about joining their group.

- The official BOTA website has more information about how to join their group.

- The AMORC website has more information about Rosicrucianism in general, including articles about their history and beliefs.

Once the candidate has met all of these requirements, they are allowed to petition for membership in one of the Rosicrucian Orders. Some groups may allow them to take a brief test before they are allowed to enter the Order. After passing all of these requirements, they are accepted as new members and invited to participate in the ceremonies that will allow them to progress from one degree to another. At this point, they are told what steps must be taken before they will be allowed to progress on to the next degree.

Conclusion

What we've learned in this section is that we can see the originators and founders of the Rosicrucian Order were all Kabbalistic Hermetists, and thus they brought with them a significant influence from Alchemy and Merkavah Mysticism. The Rosicrucian Order is an astral magic order posited on mystical Judaism and Christianity. Several of the founders were Jewish Kabbalists, while several others were Christian mystics. All of these came together to create a mélange that makes up modern Rosicrucianism (and Freemasonry).

While it is true that there are some differences between the Kabbalah and the Merkavah, if you look at it closely enough, they can appear to be the same. This is mainly because Kabbalah has its roots in Merkavah, and the way that the doctrines of the Kabbalah were set down was through a book called Sefer Yetzirah - which is a guide to meditating on mystical Jewish Mysticism. The concepts of the spiritual underworld and Chakra systems are also very similar in both Kabbalah, Alchemy, and Merkavah. The Astral Body, the Seat of the Soul, and the Plane of Yetzirah are all part of this mystical system.

This guide has been created as a primer for those who would like to go further and delve deeper into the Rosicrucians and Esoteric Christianity teachings. We have tried to give you enough information so you can go off and find out more on this topic if you are interested.

In the first chapter, we outlined Rosicrucianism properly for you and have given you some insight into the original Rosicrucian Order. In the second chapter, we talked about who Christian Rosenkreuz was and the history of the Rosicrucian Order.

The third chapter covered the Mysteries of Hermes, and the fourth chapter went over Poimandres, a Gnostic text. The fifth chapter looked at the mystical system of Merkavah, including the various levels of heaven and their correspondences in the Kabbalistic Tree of Life. The sixth went over the Twenty-Two Paths of Enlightenment as well as the mystical journeys of the path and much more. The seventh chapter covered Alchemy and Kabbalah, looking at Yesod, Hod, and Netzach in the Kabbalistic tree of life. The eighth chapter is about practical Rosicrucianism and how to practice this system of mystical Judaism.

The ninth chapter covered the daily life of a Rosicrucian as well as many other important topics in great depth. In the Bonus chapters, we have given you some insight into the secret signs of the Rosicrucians as well as a quick guide to becoming a Rosicrucian. Finally, we have included a list of further reading for the serious student.

All of this has been a small glimpse into the complicated world of Rosicrucianism and Hermeticism. This guide has been created so that you can go out and further your knowledge in this field if you're so inclined. We have tried to give a solid foundation in Rosicrucianism and its related branches of Kabbalah, Alchemy, and Merkavah Mysticism. We hope that you found this guide to be educational, informative, and interesting as well as entertaining!

Here's another book by Mari Silva that you might like

Your Free Gift (only available for a limited time)

Thanks for getting this book! If you want to learn more about various spirituality topics, then join Mari Silva's community and get a free guided meditation MP3 for awakening your third eye. This guided meditation mp3 is designed to open and strengthen ones third eye so you can experience a higher state of consciousness. Simply visit the link below the image to get started.

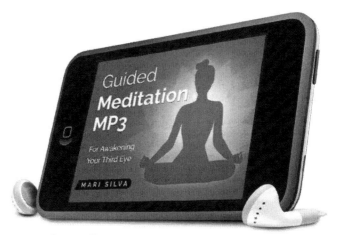

https://spiritualityspot.com/meditation

References

Goodrick-Clarke, N. (2008). Rosicrucianism. In The Western Esoteric Traditions (pp. 107–130). Oxford University Press.

Gordon Melton, J. (2020). Rosicrucian. In Encyclopedia Britannica.

Kameleon. (n.d.). A short history and introduction to the Rosicrucians. Pangeaproductions.Org. Retrieved from https://pangeaproductions.org/a-short-history-and-introduction-to-the-rosicrucians

Rosicrucians. (n.d.). Encyclopedia.Com. Retrieved from https://www.encyclopedia.com/philosophy-and-religion/other-religious-beliefs-and-general-terms/miscellaneous-religion/rosicrucians

The origins of Rosicrucianism. (2020, August 8). The Great Courses Daily. https://www.thegreatcoursesdaily.com/the-origins-of-rosicrucianism

What is Rosicrucianism, introduction in various languages and Dialects. (n.d.). AMORC. Retrieved from https://www.amorc.org/rosicrucianism

Alec nevala-lee. (n.d.). Alec Nevala-Lee. Retrieved from https://nevalalee.wordpress.com/tag/christian-rosenkreuz/

Anonymous, & Andreae, J. V. (2014). Chymical Wedding of Christian Rosenkreutz. Lulu.com. https://www.gohd.com.sg/shop/the-chymical-wedding-of-christian-rosenkreutz

Christian Rosenkreuz Explained. (n.d.). Explained.Today. Retrieved from https://everything.explained.today/Christian_Rosenkreuz

Christian_rosenkreuz. (n.d.). Chemeurope.Com. Retrieved from https://www.chemeurope.com/en/encyclopedia/Christian_Rosenkreuz.html

Westcott, W. W. (n.d.). Christian Rosenkreuz and the Rosicrucians. Website-Editor.Net. Retrieved from https://cdn.website-editor.net/e4d6563c50794969b714ab70457d9761/files/uploaded/Siftings_V6_A15a.pdf

Ebeling, F. (2007). The secret history of Hermes trismegistus: Hermeticism from ancient to modern times (D. Lorton, Trans.). Cornell University Press.

Empyreance IX - mysteries of Hermes the divine - learn online. (n.d.). Drdemartini.Com. Retrieved from https://drdemartini.com/learn/course/44/empyreance-ix-mysteries-of-hermes-the-divine

Hermes Trismegistos: Erkenntnis der Natur und des sich darin offenbarenden grossen Gottes. Begriffen in 17 unterschiedlichen Büchern nach griechischen und lateinischen Exemplaren in die Hochdeutsche übersetzet. (1997). EDIS.

Product details. (2019, April 2). Cornell University Press. https://www.cornellpress.cornell.edu/book/9780801445460/the-secret-history-of-hermes-trismegistus

The secret history of Hermes Trismegistus: hermeticism from ancient to modern times. (2008). Choice (Chicago, Ill.), 45(05), 45-2549-45-2549. https://doi.org/10.5860/choice.45-2549

Poimandres - Hermetica. (n.d.). Stjohnsem.Edu. Retrieved from

http://ldysinger.stjohnsem.edu/@texts/0301_corp_herm/01_poimandr
es.htm

Poimandres—corpus hermeticum I. (n.d.). Themathesontrust.Org.
Retrieved from

https://www.themathesontrust.org/library/poimandres-corpus-
hermeticum-i

The corpus hermeticum: I. poemandres, the Shepherd of Men.
(n.d.). Gnosis.Org. Retrieved from
http://gnosis.org/library/hermes1.html

Halperin, D. J. (n.d.). Descenders to the merkavah. Full-Stop.Net.
Retrieved from

https://www.full-stop.net/2020/06/25/blog/davidjhalperin/descenders-
to-the-merkavah

Merkabah Mysticism or Ma'aseh Merkavah. (n.d.).
Encyclopedia.Com. Retrieved from
https://www.encyclopedia.com/religion/encyclopedias-almanacs-
transcripts-and-maps/merkabah-mysticism-or-maaseh-merkavah

Merkavah Mysticism. (n.d.). Encyclopedia.Com. Retrieved from

https://www.encyclopedia.com/environment/encyclopedias-almanacs-
transcripts-and-maps/merkavah-mysticism

Robinson, G. (2002, November 15). Merkavah mysticism: The
chariot and the chamber. My Jewish Learning.
https://www.myjewishlearning.com/article/merkavah-mysticism-the-
chariot-and-the-chamber

The Editors of Encyclopedia Britannica. (2020). Merkava. In
Encyclopedia Britannica.

Avad_S. (2017, November 11). Sefirot/Emanations, Kabbalah.
Sanctum Of Magick | Aminoapps.Com.
https://aminoapps.com/c/sanctumofmagick/page/blog/sefirot-
emanations-
kabbalah/bN4v_bGDhou0MbKgw2ENqLWoZx3vqYd7dNK

Kabbalah and Healing :: Teachings :: Tree of life. (n.d.).
Kabbalahandhealing.Com. Retrieved from
http://www.kabbalahandhealing.com/tree-of-life.html

The Emanations — angelarium: The Encyclopedia of Angels. (n.d.).
Angelarium: The Encyclopedia of Angels. Retrieved from
https://www.angelarium.net/treeoflife

Are alchemy and kabbalah related? (n.d.). Quora. Retrieved from
https://www.quora.com/Are-alchemy-and-kabbalah-related

Avad_S. (2017, November 11). Sefirot/Emanations, Kabbalah.
Sanctum Of Magick | Aminoapps.Com.
https://aminoapps.com/c/sanctumofmagick/page/blog/sefirot-
emanations-
kabbalah/bN4v_bGDhou0MbKgw2ENqLWoZx3vqYd7dNK

Bos, G. (n.d.). I:Iayyim vital's "practical kabbalah and alchemy": A
17th century book of secrets. Brill.Com. Retrieved from
https://brill.com/previewpdf/journals/jjtp/4/1/article-p55_4.xml

Kabbalah and Healing :: Teachings :: Tree of life. (n.d.).
Kabbalahandhealing.Com. Retrieved from
http://www.kabbalahandhealing.com/tree-of-life.html

Ottmann, K. (n.d.). Alchemy and kabbalah : Scholem, Gershom
Gerhard, Ottmann, Klaus: Amazon.In: Books. Amazon.In. Retrieved
from https://www.amazon.in/Alchemy-Kabbalah-Gershom-Gerhard-
Scholem/dp/0882145665

Sefirot - tree of Life. (n.d.). Geneseo.Edu. Retrieved from
https://www.geneseo.edu/yoga/sefirot-tree-life

The Emanations — angelarium: The Encyclopedia of Angels. (n.d.).
Angelarium: The Encyclopedia of Angels. Retrieved from
https://www.angelarium.net/treeoflife

Atkinson, W. W. (2017). The secret doctrines of the Rosicrucians - E-
book - William Walker Atkinson - storytel. Musaicum Books.

Holt, D. (2018, May 5). How to practice rosicrucianism. Phoenix Esoteric Society. https://phoenixesotericsociety.com/how-to-practice-rosicrucianism

On the practical paths of rosicrucianism. (n.d.). Futureconscience.Com. Retrieved from https://www.futureconscience.com/the-practical-paths-of-rosicrucianism

Rosicrucians. (n.d.). Encyclopedia.Com. Retrieved from https://www.encyclopedia.com/philosophy-and-religion/other-religious-beliefs-and-general-terms/miscellaneous-religion/rosicrucians

The origins of rosicrucianism. (2020, August 8). The Great Courses Daily. https://www.thegreatcoursesdaily.com/the-origins-of-rosicrucianism

Acher, F. (2020, October 10). Rosicrucian Magic. A manifest. Theomagica. https://theomagica.com/blog/rosicrucian-magic-a-manifest

Amorc, O. (2020, February 1). Three daily Rosicrucian practices to boost your energy, health, and happiness. Rosicrucians In Oregon. https://rosicruciansinportlandoregonwilsonville.com/2020/02/01/three-daily-rosicrucian-practices-to-boost-you-energy-health-and-happiness

Armstrong, S. (n.d.). daily routine – Podcasts. Rosicrucian.Org. Retrieved from https://www.rosicrucian.org/podcast/tag/daily-routine

Rosicrucian code of life. (n.d.). The Rosicrucian Order, AMORC. Retrieved from https://www.rosicrucian.org/rosicrucian-code-of-life

Rosicrucians. (n.d.). Encyclopedia.Com. Retrieved from https://www.encyclopedia.com/philosophy-and-religion/other-religious-beliefs-and-general-terms/miscellaneous-religion/rosicrucians

The origins of rosicrucianism. (2020, August 8). The Great Courses Daily.

https://www.thegreatcoursesdaily.com/the-origins-of-rosicrucianism

17th Century Anon. (2011a). Secret symbols of the rosicrucians. Lulu.com.

https://www.rosicrucian.org/secret-symbols-of-the-rosicrucians

17th Century Anon. (2011b). Secret symbols of the rosicrucians. Lulu.com.

http://www.levity.com/alchemy/secret_s.html

Franz Hartmann - The Secret Signs of the Rosicrucians. (2015, August 2). HERMETICS. https://www.hermetics.net/media-library/rosicrucianism/franz-hartmann-the-secret-signs-of-the-rosicrucians/

(N.d.). Bookshop.Org. Retrieved from https://bookshop.org/books/rosicrucian-rules-secret-signs-codes-and-symbols-esoteric-classics/9781631184888

Become a Member. (2006). IEEE Transactions on Mobile Computing, 5(5), 608–608.

https://doi.org/10.1109/tmc.2006.56

Become a Rosicrucian Student. (n.d.). The Rosicrucian Order, AMORC. Retrieved from

https://www.rosicrucian.org/become-a-student

Gordon Melton, J. (2020). Rosicrucian. In Encyclopedia Britannica.

How do you join the Rosicrucians? And how can you tell if your being recruited? (n.d.). Quora. Retrieved from https://www.quora.com/How-do-you-join-the-Rosicrucians-And-how-can-you-tell-if-your-being-recruited

Made in the USA
Middletown, DE
31 August 2024